D0898045

THE CULTIVATION OF ARTISTS
IN NINETEENTH-CENTURY AMERICA

The Cultivation of Artists in Nineteenth-Century America

EDITED BY
GEORGIA BRADY BARNHILL,
DIANA KORZENIK, AND CAROLINE F. SLOAT

WORCESTER, MASSACHUSETTS
AMERICAN ANTIQUARIAN SOCIETY
1997

The contents of this book also appear in the *Proceedings of the American Antiquarian Society*, Volume 105, part 1, April 1995.

The Society gratefully acknowledges the generosity of The Heald Foundation in the publication of this volume.

ISBN 0-944026-75-3

LIBRARY OF CONGRESS CATALOGUING-IN-PUBLICATION DATA

The cultivation of artists in nineteenth-century America / edited by George Brady Barnhill, Diana Korzenik, and Caroline F. Sloat.
    p.   cm.
"Proceedings of a conference held at the American Antiquarian Society, April 30–May 2, 1993."
Includes bibliographical references and index.
ISBN 0-944026-75-3 (hardcover : alk. paper)
    1. Artists—Training of—United States—History—19th century—Congresses.   I. Barnhill, Georgia Brady, 1944–   . II. Korzenik, Diana, 1941–   . III. Sloat, Caroline.   IV. American Antiquarian Society.
N107.C86   1997
707'.1'073—dc21   97-4458
                                                      CIP

PRINTED IN THE UNITED STATES OF AMERICA

The paper used in this publication meets the minimum requirements of American National Standard for Information Sciences—Permanence of Paper for Printed Library Materials, ANSI Z39.48–1984.

Table of Contents

*The Cultivation of Artists in
Nineteenth-Century America*

Preface

GEORGIA B. BARNHILL

O N BEHALF OF the American Antiquarian Society, it is my pleasure to express our gratitude to those who made the symposium and publication possible. Sinclair Hitchings, Keeper of Prints at the Boston Public Library, David F. Tatham, Professor of Fine Arts at Syracuse University, and Diana Korzenik, formerly of the Massachusetts College of Art, made substantial contributions to the shape and content of the symposium. The symposium was underwritten in part by donations from The Heald Foundation, The Dave H. and Reba Williams Foundation, Ronald S. Davis, and Leonard Milberg. Additional support from The Heald Foundation has made the publication of the papers possible. Caroline F. Sloat, editor of publications at the American Antiquarian Society, edited the papers with sensitivity and enthusiasm.

In part, the symposium was a celebration of the gift of the Cross Family Art Archive to the American Antiquarian Society by Diana Korzenik. This remarkable collection of works by three siblings from Manchester, New Hampshire, Henry Clay Cross, Joel Foster Cross, and Emma Cross, includes examples of their childhood drawings and instructional works, as well as proofs of their wood engravings, oils, and watercolors done as adults. In 1995 the collection was augmented by the thoughtful gift of Mrs. Elizabeth Cross of additional art works, sketch

GEORGIA B. BARNHILL is the Andrew W. Mellon curator of graphic arts at the American Antiquarian Society.

books, photographs, and family memorabilia. The Society also purchased the collection of letters written by the children's father during his military service during the Civil War. Like Diana Korzenik, Mrs. Cross realized the importance of keeping the works of the family together in a research institution where scholars in many disciplines can use this uncommon collection.

Introduction

DIANA KORZENIK

I T IS IMPORTANT that the papers in this volume, *The Cultivation of Artists in Nineteenth-Century America*, are now bound together. They were first heard as lectures presented on two beautiful spring days on the last day of May and the first of June in 1993 to a gathering of educators, curators, artists, collectors, librarians, and scholars across disciplines. The slide-illustrated lectures were accounts of new research on the importance to American art of young artists' early formal and informal education. These papers brought to light subjects usually left in the dark.

That this symposium ever happened was due to Georgia Barnhill's enthusiastic response to an idea I proposed: a conference that focused scholarly attention on an array of early art educational experiences of American artists in different eras and of different areas within the United States. I knew the power of this material. Having taught the history of American art education, I have guided generations of students through research projects helping them form questions and find the primary source documents to investigate them in order to unravel how a certain artist got his or her start. What has emerged is a picture of the many routes to art in this country.

The symposium concept I presented to Georgia Barnhill grew from my own curiosity and gaps in my own knowledge. Since I

DIANA KORZENIK, author of *Drawn to Art* and *Artmaking and Education*, has focused her research on the history of American art education. She has taught in the New York City public schools, Massachusetts College of Art, and Harvard Graduate School of Education.

had concentrated my attention on the history of art education in schools and only through research for *Drawn to Art* had I looked at wood engravers' training, I hoped this conference could be an occasion to branch out.[1] I proposed this be an occasion for a team of interdisciplinary scholars to look at how young artists in urban centers learned on the job, how artists acquired commercial marketable skills, and how they incorporated these into their own work.

This symposium seemed timely. Over the last twenty-five years, scholars had time to integrate the certain key works influencing our conceptions of art education in this country, particularly those by Peter Marzio, Carl Dreppard, Roger Stein, Lois Marie Fink and Joshua Taylor, Lillian Miller, and Neil Harris.[2]

Meanwhile key works in other fields also influenced the interpretation of the history of American art education. Sociologist Howard Becker's *Art Worlds* opened an entirely other sort of discussion.[3] He demonstrated that the artist is and has been an artifact of hosts of supporting players. The gallery directors, framers, the agents, publicists, patrons, critics, art shippers, and teachers are all parts of a vast social system with certain social agreements. Collectively their extensive labors promote the illusion of a sole master. From another field, psychology, Rudolf Arnheim, particularly in *Visual Thinking* showed the normalcy of artistic thinking.[4] If visual conception is built into all of us, then instruction either closes down or opens up normal mental functioning. From the field of American studies, Eileen Boris in *Art and Labor* looked at different conceptions of art-making as labor, from the English

1. Diana Korzenik, *Drawn to Art: A Nineteenth-Century American Dream* (Hanover, N.H.: University Press of New England, 1985).

2. Peter Marzio, *The Art Crusade* (Washington: Smithsonian Institution Press, 1976); Carl Dreppard, *American Drawing Books* (New York: New York Public Library, 1946); Neil Harris, *The Artist in American Society* (New York: George Braziller, 1966); Roger B. Stein, *John Ruskin and Aesthetic Thought in America, 1840–1900* (Cambridge: Harvard University Press, 1967); Lois Marie Fink and Joshua Taylor, *Academy: The Academic Tradition in American Art* (Washington, D.C.: Smithsonian Institution Press, 1975); and Lillian B. Miller, *Patrons and Patriotism: The Encouragement of Fine Arts in the United States, 1790–1860* (Chicago: University of Chicago Press, 1966).

3. Howard S. Becker, *Art Worlds* (Berkeley: University of California Press, 1982).

4. Rudolf Arnheim, *Visual Thinking* (London: Faber and Faber, 1969).

craftsman ideal to the schooling of taste in the American public school to women's culture joining art and philanthropy.[5]

In the past decade historians within the field of art education—Foster Wygant, Arthur Efland, and I—have generated quite a few books on art education history.[6] Three thematically related volumes of historical studies are Enid Zimmerman and Mary Ann Stankiewicz, *Women Art Educators, Women Art Educators II*, and Kristin Cogdon and Zimmerman, *Women Art Educators III*.[7] The National Art Education Association has supported this research movement publishing the collected papers from two international conferences at Pennsylvania State University in 1985 (Wilson and Hoffa), and in 1989, as well as a Canadian, British, and American retrospective in *Framing the Past*.[8]

A planning committee—Sinclair Hitchings, David Tatham, Georgia Barnhill, and I—developed several thematic questions: To what extent were artists trained in-house, in quasi-apprenticeships? Was such training replaced by pre-employment and extra-employment in schools such as the Rhode Island School of Design? Did art schools ultimately replace workshops? A call for papers went out to scholars in several disciplines announcing that the conference 'will explore how nineteenth-century businesses offered training opportunities. Because of economic necessity,

5. Eileen C. Boris, *Art and Labor: John Ruskin, William Morris and the Craftsman Ideal in America* ([Providence]: Brown University, 1986).

6. Foster Wygant, *School Art in American Culture, 1820–1970* (Cincinnati: Interwood Press, 1993); *Standards for Art Teacher Preparation Programs* (Reston, Va.: National Art Education Association, c. 1990); and *Art in American Schools in the Nineteenth Century* (Cincinnati: Interwood Press, 1993); Arthur Efland, *A History of Art Education* (New York: Teachers College, Columbia University, 1990); and Diana Korzenik and Maurice Brown, *Art Making and Education* (Urbana: University of Illinois Press, 1993).

7. Enid Zimmerman and Mary Ann Stankiewicz, *Women Art Educators* (Bloomington: Department of Art Education, Indiana University, 1982) and *Women Art Educators II* (Bloomington: Department of Art Education, Indiana University, 1985); and Kristin Cogdon and Enid Zimmerman, *Women Art Educators III* (Bloomington: Department of Art Education, Indiana University, 1993).

8. Brent Wilson and Harland Hoffa, *The History of Art Education: Proceedings from the Pennsylvania State University Conference* (Reston, Va.: National Art Education Association, 1985); Patricia M. Amburgy, ed., *The History of Art Education* (Reston, Va.: National Art Education Association, 1992); Donald Soucy and Mary Ann Stankiewicz, eds., *Framing the Past* (Reston, Va.: National Art Education Association, 1990).

numbers of young people sought employment in the shops of commercial pictorial printmakers and publishers.' It raised some questions: 'What were the patterns and processes through which artists entered their trade? What were the expectations of the employers? How did they help young people to meet them? How did pictorial printing firms shelter, nurture, and train new generations of artists?' The idea was to focus on the company climate of different graphic art firms located in urban centers in nineteenth-century America.

From the responses that came in, it became obvious that the symposium presentations could not present workplaces without also discussing schools. The papers particularly related to the 1870s and 1880s highlighted how intertwined were the developments of formal art classes and employment opportunities. The Massachusetts legislature's 1870 Drawing Act conceived the mission of schools and jobs in tandem. Art education in public day schools and publicly funded adult evening classes were expected to advance commercial textile, metals, glass, and ceramics production. So school and on-the-job training became our dual subjects.

In my mind, one objective for undertaking this symposium was to correct a pattern of art historical writing that James Flexner identified back in 1947. 'Modern art historians, determined to find what seems to them *more suitably elevated sources* [my emphasis] for the landscapists' style and achievements, have overlooked the significance of the fact that a large majority of the painters began their careers and received their basic training in the workshop of commercial engravers.'[9] Some of these 'less elevated, overlooked sources' are the young person's schooling and preparation for the many artistically-oriented trades.

What is puzzling is why it has taken fifty years for a significant number of scholars to define artistic elements in the trades. What has kept people away from these 'less elevated sources'? One rea-

9. *Asher B. Durand: An Engraver's and a Farmer's Art* (Yonkers, N.Y.: Hudson River Museum, 1983), 7.

son has to do with how art is studied and collected. An example of the problem concerned the collection of the art made by one family in New Hampshire that became the basis for my writing *Drawn to Art*. When I first found the collection, I immediately saw how much could be learned from all of it because so much of the work of the family's three artists survived together. Still together were the wood engravings produced at the Boston firm, Kilburn and Cross, with fancy leather-bound books produced using the engravings. With these were family photographs, watercolors, drawings, oil paintings on small pieces of canvas, greeting cards, ledgers, recipe books, a few woodblocks, and advertising booklets for which the Crosses engraved, as well as the ephemera the family saved that were the products of their competitors.

But when my writing using the collection was done, I needed to find the Cross archive a new home where all would continue to be kept together. Here I faced the problem. The fact is that among institutions that collect objects, mass-produced advertising and illustration work tends to be welcomed in entirely different sorts of institutions than those that preserve paintings and drawings. Art museums in many cases prefer to edit out those 'less elevated sources.' That this conference and book were sponsored by the American Antiquarian Society reflects the same generosity of spirit that makes AAS the ideal home for the *Drawn to Art* collection. Here, both conceptually and physically, the fine arts and the commercial work are welcomed together. They are understood to be parts of a larger social, intellectual, and political enterprise.

The mission of the conference was to permit the commercial and the fine arts, education, and employment, to converge where they do in order to uncover American patterns. One example is Flexner's thesis that American art is a working-class art, that it is a tradesperson's art. 'Painting is not an upper-class tradition superimposed from above, but an extension of artisans engaged in utilitarian tasks.'[10] We hoped the papers might show how in this

10. James T. Flexner, *American Painting. The First Flowers of Our Wilderness* (Boston: Houghton, Mifflin, 1947), 6–7.

country, though not necessarily by law or policy, art has been made accessible to many classes and subcultures. In a letter after the conference, in the spirit of Flexner, Elizabeth Hawkes observed: 'The conference brought up an overlooked point. In the nineteenth century young people with artistic aspirations from the lower and middle class could not afford traditional art school training and study in Europe. Some businesses (such as printing and publishing companies), for example, provided an alternative entry to art education. This is certainly the case for some of the Ashcan artists who got their start in the newspaper and magazine business.' In this vein Donald O'Brien's paper describes the workshop of Abner Reed, Ann Wagner documents wood engraver Hiram Merrill, and Elizabeth Hawkes shows the influence of a newspaper artist's training on the art of John Sloan. Florence Jumonville traces the lithography of New Orleans sheet music by Henri and Clementine Wehrmann. Serendipitously the paper about the drawings at the New Orleans Notarial Archives delivered by Sally Reeves at the American Antiquarian Society's semi-annual meeting in April 1995 continued the theme of art education in the Crescent City. Reeves's description of the plan-book drawings complements Jumonville's essay and furthers the discussion of on-the-job training as art education.

In addition to the artisan tradition, we also have had a far-reaching system of democratization of art: the local public school. Elliot Davis's work on Fitz Hugh Lane shows how Lane used art instruction textbooks, particularly John Gadsby Chapman's *American Drawing Book*, to develop his way of painting, among other things, sailing vessels and shadows. The changing textbooks for the curriculum in public schools' visual art education are essential reading for students of American art. The commercial art textbook producer of greatest impact and scale was Boston's Louis Prang & Company. Michael Clapper's paper 'Art, Industry, and Education in Prang's Chromolithograph Company' addresses the way in which that company exploited both the school and home market in chromolithographic art reproductions.

Other types of schools beyond the ever-expanding public school movement played critical roles in art education. One is the museum school, a professional school formally attached to fine art museums. Joyce W. Lehmann's paper traces the origins of what she called 'this hybrid institution.' Nancy Austin's paper on the industrial origins of the Rhode Island School of Design looks at one of these institutions.

All of the authors' findings testify to the fact that for art to have been passed along from one generation to another, places had to exist where young people could get their start. In any era, in order for young people to have become artists they need to have had teachers who were engaged with the forms of art current in their time. Though obviously families were of enormous importance, their role was outside the province of this symposium. What proved to be central to all these papers was the importance of some form of teaching either in schools or at workplaces. Someone had to point the young person to picture galleries, libraries, and stores selling drawing, painting, and printing materials and actually show the young person what to do to make images.

In appreciating the results of this symposium, it seems worthy to note that in our century educators and psychologists, not historians, have dominated the discussion of how young people became artists. Though art-making hardly is just about learning how to draw, often that has been the psychologists' beginning point. Their theories have agreed that a person's representation of the world on a flat piece of paper is a learned process, but they disagree about how it is learned. Most theories of how drawing is learned can be organized under one or two rubrics. One account is developmental. It posits predictable stages of a young person's artistic development. As Rousseau did two centuries ago, these twentieth-century psychologically-oriented writers describe artistic development as the unfolding of natural stages through which the growing child may be expected to pass.

The other theoretical direction looks at the students' frame of reference in learning to draw. They look at where the students direct their attention. Ernst Gombrich, James J. Gibson, and Rudolf Arnheim each have offered different accounts of this, and different pedagogy has been created from each premise. One encourages copying, while the others oppose it. One requires observational drawing, while the other concentrates the students' visual attention inward. Though the controversy has been productive particularly of instructional strategies, it seems to have denied the importance of the young art learner's own era and own local culture.

I am delighted that the papers in *The Cultivation of Artists in Nineteenth-Century America* bring the discussion of the beginnings of art back into the domain of history. To truly understand artistic development, I believe we need to know the historical particulars. Although the psychological discussion could not help but be an influence, the gold mine of historical sources, documents, correspondence, old newspapers, school circulars, curriculum reports, art instruction books, drawing cards and students' copies of them, and treatises all inform current research.

It is with great pleasure that I thank the American Antiquarian Society for expressing its commitment to these issues in this very concrete form and for seeing that the symposium papers became a publication. Thanks, too, to the members of the conference planning committee who foresaw the potential in this theme.

Training in the Workshop of Abner Reed

DONALD C. O'BRIEN

WHEN John C. Pease and John M. Niles compiled and published their *Gazetteer of the States of Connecticut and Rhode Island* in 1819, they noted that East Windsor, Connecticut, was a small community with slightly over 3,000 inhabitants. Most of these people farmed the fertile soil adjacent to the Connecticut River and lived along the main street, which ran about one mile back and parallel to the mighty watercourse. Pease and Niles also listed numerous commercial businesses that residents operated in addition to farming; these included 'six Gin Distilleries . . . one Segar Manufactory . . . and one extensive and elegant Engraving Establishment.'[1]

Documentation for this study appears essentially in three sources. The first, the unpublished diary of John Warner Barber, is at the New Haven Colony Historical Society. Hereafter, it will be cited simply as Barber followed by the date of entry. The other two sources were compiled by the grandson of Abner Reed and the son of Samuel Stiles, Henry Reed Stiles, M.D. The 'Stiles Family Memorial,' on file at the Connecticut Historical Society, is a compilation of family records—letters, trade cards, specimens of bank notes and other copperplate engravings, pictures, etc.—extending through three generations. The 'Memorial' is arranged in four volumes [boxes] and each piece has a page number. It will be cited in this work as SFM, volume, and page number. Finally, there is Henry R. Stiles, *The History and Genealogies of Ancient Windsor, Connecticut, 1635–1891*, 2 vols. (Hartford: Case, Lockwood & Brainard Company, 1891–92), cited as Stiles, volume, and page number. For this study, I have used the facsimile printed by The New Hampshire Publishing Company in 1976. This published source was compiled through letters and other personal records as well as actual conversations with individuals involved. This work will be cited as Stiles, volume, and page number.

    1. John C. Pease and John M. Niles, *A Gazetteer of the States of Connecticut and Rhode Island* (Hartford: William S. Marsh, 1819), 65–67. The part of East Windsor where Abner Reed lived was incorporated as South Windsor in 1845.

DONALD C. O'BRIEN edits the *Newsletter* for the American Historical Print Collectors Society. He is also an adjunct faculty member in history at Oakland Community College, Auburn Hills, Michigan.

This 'extensive and elegant engraving establishment' was the 'large and well-fitted workshop' of Abner Reed, 'wherein he executed all kinds of jobs in wood and metal, with rare and even tedious accuracy.' He moved his business from Hartford to a location '30 rods south of the meeting house, first society' in the summer of 1811 and remained there for nearly two decades. His shop was located in the second story of an addition running east from his house on the main street. Another addition was made to the north side during the summer of 1818.[2]

Abner Reed was a transitional figure in American engraving. Trained in the older craft tradition and not satisfied with the old ways, Reed was one of those 'Yankee Dreamers and Doers,' described by Ellsworth Strong Grant,[3] who continually sought progress through technological change. He was a pioneer in experimenting with aquatint, and his work in bank note engraving is well known. Reed also trained many of the men who built the great commercial engraving establishments of the mid-nineteenth century. The apprenticeship opportunities offered by Reed were probably not unique, but they are exceptionally well documented.

Born in East Windsor in November 1771, Reed was ninety-four when he died in Toledo, Ohio, in February 1866. His education consisted of a few years in the district school learning the rudiments of reading, writing, spelling, and some arithmetic. At the age of fourteen and in his final year of school, Reed learned the basics of calligraphy by copying German and Old English texts onto paper. This training was extremely helpful and Reed's innate ability can be readily detected in his completed engravings.[4]

After finishing his formal education in 1786, Reed entered into

2. See the announcement in the *Connecticut Mirror*, July 29, 1811, 3:5. A good description of the property is found in Stiles, 2: 635. Barber recorded moving into the new shop, September 16, 1818.

3. Ellsworth Strong Grant, *Yankee Dreamers and Doers* (Chester, Conn.: Pequot Press, [1978]).

4. For a biographical sketch, see Stiles, 2: 634–37 and my article 'Abner Reed: A Connecticut Engraver,' *The Connecticut Historical Society Bulletin* 44 (January 1979): 1–16.

an apprenticeship with Samuel May, a local saddler and harness maker whose son Charles, seven years Reed's senior, may have taught him the trade. Perhaps they even became friends working side by side, as Charles married Reed's sister Chloe in 1795. While working for the Mays, Reed saw future possibilities for work when observing saddles with engraved plates with the maker's name brought into the shop for repairs. Sometime, probably late in his apprenticeship, he started to use his skills in calligraphy by engraving his own saddle plates. Copper was obtained locally at least once, for the local clockmaker, Daniel Burnap, noted in his account book in April 1791, 'Mr. Charls [sic] May to One Copper plate for Abner Reed.'[5]

When Reed finished his apprenticeship in 1793, he moved to Lansingburgh, New York. This small river community just north of Albany on the east side of the Hudson had attracted many settlers from East Windsor. Quickly Reed found employment teaching school and began his graphic art career by engraving illustrations on copper for area printers. He married Elizabeth Loring in 1795 and they had six children. She died in 1854 after nearly sixty years of marriage.

Sometime in 1797 at his father's request, Reed and his wife returned to East Windsor. He continued to teach school, but according to his carefully kept diary he expanded his business to include 'Painting, engraving bank notes, printing, graining chairs, lettering coffins, cartridges, boxes, engraving frontispieces and farming.'[6] The diary indicates that he suffered from an erratic income, but eventually bank note engraving became his primary source of cash. At the time Reed also joined the Congregational Church and was soon elected a deacon, a position he maintained for nearly fifty years, and a title he preferred to have used.

5. Cited in Penrose R. Hoopes, *Shop Records of Daniel Burnap, Clockmaker* ([Hartford]: The Connecticut Historical Society, 1958), 21.
6. Unpublished manuscript on file at The Connecticut Historical Society. For a description of the diary, see Thompson R. Harlow, 'Connecticut Engravers, 1774–1820,' *The Connecticut Historical Society Bulletin* 36 (October 1971): 111–12.

Toward the end of 1803 Reed moved his shop to Hartford, a city which had become a significant publishing and printing center by the early nineteenth century. He advertised in the *American Mercury* that he was engaged in 'Copperplate & Typographical Engraving, Rolling-Press Printing, Sign Painting, Gilding, etc.' In the same advertisement, he stated that he was looking for 'an apprentice to all or any of the above branches, a Lad of from 14 to 16 or 17 years old, of good morals and bright genius.'[7] Over the years he trained a number of young men who made names for themselves as engravers.

Among the earliest apprentices was Asaph Willard (1786–1880). He became competent in the field of bank note engraving and worked for his former master on and off after completing his apprenticeship. In partnership with other engravers trained by Reed, including Ralph Rawdon (d. c. 1877), he made significant contributions in the field through the formation of various companies which improved the quality and sophistication of bank note and pictorial engraving.[8] Although Rawdon and Willard are known today for their work on copper plates, Reed also trained them in the basics of wood engraving. At a later time Reed's process of making relief cuts was described: 'The blocks of [a] pear tree at that date were coated with India Ink, the outline put on in red chalk and the picture revealed itself as the engraver progressed in his work.'[9]

Another apprentice in the Reed workshop in the first decade of the nineteenth century was William Mason (c. 1790–c. 1844). Engraving on wood became his medium after he became intrigued with the wood engravings of Alexander Anderson. After careful study he made his initial attempt in 1808 by engraving

7. Hartford, November 17, 1803, 3: 4. This advertisement is reproduced in Harlow, 'Connecticut Engravers,' 112.

8. Rawdon's link to Reed is ambiguous. Barber, August 25, 1820, noted 'R. Rawdon came,' but there is no mention of his being at the Reed residence during his apprenticeship. However, Stiles listed him as a Reed apprentice. For Willard, see his death notice in the *Providence Journal*, July 16, 1880. The same notice, somewhat abbreviated, appeared in the *American Art Review* 1 (1880): 455.

9. *Ibid.*

book illustrations. Mason moved to Philadelphia after completing his apprenticeship in 1810. Apparently he gave up engraving sometime after 1830 to become a drawing teacher.[10]

Reed also needed a plate printer, and this job fell to William Phelps (1785–1858). Little is known about Phelps or whether he ever completed an apprenticeship. However, he remained Reed's press operator for a number of years, and it was Phelps who accompanied his employer in early June 1811 to see about moving back to East Windsor, a feat accomplished the following month. Phelps became more than a simple laborer in the workshop when in 1813 he married Chloe Reed May, the daughter of Reed's late sister and Charles May, the son of Abner Reed's former master.[11]

The specific reasons for moving back to East Windsor are unknown, but several factors may have prompted Reed. Operating in Hartford had to be costlier; he probably arranged with Charles Hosmer (1785–1871), publisher of the *Connecticut Mirror*, to become his agent and stock his inventory of drawing books, school certificates, and pictures. New orders could be easily sent to East Windsor only six miles away and on a direct stage route.[12] Undoubtedly, Reed needed some farmland for his family's needs and a larger building which could provide a workshop as well as living space. The welfare of his parents may have been a major consideration, as they resided with him until their deaths a few years later.

William Phelps, as well as Asaph Willard, followed Reed across the river. Again there was a need for someone to run errands, help out with the chores, and work in the shop at assigned tasks while

10. See William Dunlap, *History of the Rise and Progress of the Arts of Design in the United States*, 2 vols. (New York, 1834; rpt. New York: Dover Publications, 1969), 2, part one: 228.

11. Sometime in 1971, a lady sent to The Connecticut Historical Society a photocopy of two leaves from a day book kept by her great-grandfather, William Phelps. These cover the periods from May 24 through June 25, 1811 and from August 10 through September 10, 1812. In addition to the entry for June 7, 1811, 'Went to EW with Mr. Reed to see about moving,' Phelps wrote on September 8, 1812, 'Helped Willard print new blocks.' Unfortunately, this woman did not include her address so CHS was unable to respond. Letter from Thompson R. Harlow, November 29, 1983, to Donald C. O'Brien. Phelps's marriage is confirmed in *Diary of Thomas Robbins, D.D. 1796–1854*, Increase N. Tarbox ed., 2 vols. (Boston: Beacon Press, 1886), 1: 550.

12. See the advertisement in the *Connecticut Mirror*, July 29, 1811, 3: 5.

learning the trade. Hence Reed started looking for young apprentices. His first choice was a son of a local elder, Captain
Asahel Stiles. When making his offer, Reed shrewdly argued, 'I
cannot think that I can make it at all advantageous to myself.'[13]
He agreed, however, to take the boy provided the father would
pay for clothing and board for the first year. Later a second son
entered the workshop. Obviously, Reed did not want to make any
investment until the young man proved himself. He continued, 'A
long time is required in learning to draw, which is absolutely necessary in the first place, and a long time to practice engraving before anything can be done at customer's work, and much time
spent in instruction, etc.'[14]

After stating that an apprenticeship required seven years, Reed
further promised '. . . to do well by him in instructing and treatment, and should we both live till his apprenticeship expires, I
shall probably be willing to give him good wages for any time he
may wish to stay with me afterwards.'[15] Stiles's son Samuel
(1796–1861) was greatly influenced by his master, but it is very
probable that his older brother, Asahel Chapin Stiles (1793–1866),
also went to Reed. If Asahel did not enter into a formal apprenticeship, he at least worked in Reed's workshop for several years.[16]

The following year Reed made another excellent choice in ac-
cepting into his shop John Warner Barber (1798–1885), the future
engraver, topographical draughtsman, and historian. Recently
left fatherless, Barber needed a guardian while Reed needed a
worker. It was an ideal solution for both. As soon as he began his apprenticeship on January 22, 1813, Barber started keeping a diary,
probably at Reed's suggestion, and continued it until his death in
1885. Although extremely cryptic and lacking description or
analysis, it gives the reader a glimpse into Barber's daily routine,
especially during the seven years of service under Abner Reed.[17]

13. SFM, 2: 69.
14. *Ibid.*
15. *Ibid.*
16. See the Stiles genealogy in Stiles, 2: 711–12.
17. For more information on Barber, see my article 'John Warner Barber: A

Barber came from Windsor on the other side of the river,[18] so it must have been a novelty in the beginning to run the errands. He went frequently to such places as the mill 'upon the Hill,' to 'Pitkin's [Glass] Factory,' and as far away as East Hartford. Chores were plentiful as well—'loading sand and dung,' 'working in the garden,' 'pitching hay,' and 'piling up wood.' During July, he was loaned out for a week to reap grain at the farm of Reed's brother. For the Sabbath, Barber simply made the notation 'Sunday' at first, but as he grew older he included biblical quotations, where he attended church, and usually the name of the preacher. Of course, there was never any mention of work on Sunday, not even chores.

Within a fortnight Barber established a pattern that lasted a lifetime. He engraved daily, usually in the morning, or he spent his time drawing—occasionally listing his subjects, beasts and birds, maps, and even 'Dr. Franklin's head.' There is no mention of what he was engraving at this initial stage so it can be assumed that he was simply practicing. Whether he received direct instruction is also unknown; perhaps he was expected to teach himself by observation and practice, and his instruction was limited to casual suggestions from his master.

Barber also learned the dirtier side of the trade as 'The copperplates were taken in the rough sheet, hammered, stoned, polished and burnished by the young men.'[19] These were tasks frequently mentioned in the diary. He was also printing—'Helped Mr. Phelps print bank bills,' 'Printed watch cards,' 'Printed certificates,' or 'Printing Washington 1000 [copies].' At the same

---

Connecticut Engraver,' *Imprint* 4 (April 1979), 20–22; Richard Hegel, *Nineteenth-Century Historians of New Haven* (Hamden, Connecticut: Archon Books, 1972), 32–50; Chauncey C. Nash, 'John Warner Barber and his Books,' *Walpole Society Note Book* (1934) 5–35; Henry H. Townshend, 'John Warner Barber, Illustrator and Historian,' *Papers of the New Haven Colony Historical Society* 10 (1951): 313–36; and Christopher P. Bickford and J. Bard McNulty eds., *John Warner Barber's Views of Connecticut Towns, 1834–1836* ([Hartford]: The Acorn Club, [1990]).

18. It has often been stated that Barber was born in East Windsor, but Stiles, 2: 54, shows that his father Elijah resided in Windsor and that is where his mother lived throughout his apprenticeship.

19. *Providence Journal*, July 16, 1880.

time, he was binding and trimming copies, or 'colouring clock faces' and 'painting frontispieces.'

Barber also noted exceptions to his routine. For example, he visited his family about six times a year. When allowed to go home, he generally left on Saturday afternoon, spent Sunday with his family, and returned Monday morning. In the beginning he usually went directly home across the river by Bissell's Ferry; as he grew older, however, he sometimes 'Returned by Hartford 17 miles' as he did on Christmas Day 1815. Sometimes he tarried in Hartford and spent his time there attending religious meetings or going to the museum.[20]

He also recorded the comings and goings of household help. The Reed household was probably in need of continual help providing for six children plus the apprentices in Mrs. Reed's care. Abner Reed's guests were also noted in the diary. On May 11, 1813, Barber wrote that 'Mr. Kensett and his wife came.' No doubt this was the engraver, Thomas Kensett (1786–1829), a partner in the firm of Shelton & Kensett, map and print publishers, and father of John Frederick Kensett (1816–72), landscape painter and engraver.

It has been assumed that Ralph Rawdon worked for Shelton & Kensett because his engraving, *Col. Johnsons mounted men charging a party of British Artillerists & Indians, at the Battle fought near Moravian Town October 2nd 1813*, was published and sold by Shelton & Kensett of Cheshire, Connecticut, in 1813 (fig. 1). This may not be the case, because Barber noted in September that 'Ralph got home' and a week later he wrote 'Printing certificates with Ralph.' These entries lead one to believe that Rawdon did the actual engraving in Reed's workshop. Hence Reed may have been doing business with Shelton & Kensett all along, and the Kensetts' visit that spring may have been for business reasons.

In his seven years at the Reed household, Barber mentioned

20. Undoubtedly this was the museum of Joseph Steward (1753–1822), portrait painter and silhouettist. See Thompson R. Harlow, 'The Versatile Joseph Steward, Portrait Painter and Museum Proprietor,' *Antiques* 121 (January 1982): 303–11.

Fig. 1. Col. Johnsons mounted men charging a party of British Artillerists & Indians, at the Battle fought near Moravian Town October 2nd 1813. when the whole of the British force commanded by Gen. Procter, surrendered to the Army under Gen. Harrison and his gallant followers. Published and sold by Shelton & Kensett Con. Dec 6th 1813. Engraved by R. Rawdon. The Connecticut Historical Society, Hartford, Connecticut.

reading only three books, which is probably not a reflection on his interest but merely an indication of the limited amount of reading material in circulation at the time. Of course, his reading would have been enhanced by the reading of scripture in church and by the numerous materials to be engraved and printed that went through the Reed workshop.[21]

The second year into his apprenticeship found Barber no longer running errands; obviously there was a younger boy in the workshop fulfilling this task. However, he was still responsible for many chores. Often he commented that he worked in the garden or became more specific by remarking, 'hoed beans,' 'raking hay

21. Barber, March 24–31, 1813, 'Reading Stranger in Ireland,' July 25, 1817, 'Reading The Christian Memoir,' and March 15, 1818, 'Read Cotton Mather's Life.'

Fig. 2. *The Georgia Militia under Gen. Floyd attacking the Creek Indians at Autosee –Novr 29th 1813. Published by W. Phelps & Co. E. Windsor Con. March 1814.* The Connecticut Historical Society, Hartford, Connecticut.

with Asahel in the meadow,' 'picking over potatoes,' or 'went after walnuts.'

Barber was now engraving daily with intermittent breaks, and occasionally he revealed his subject matter. New Year's Day of 1814 found him engraving a Washington plate which was probably one of the two different engravings of the first President produced by Reed. Over the winter Barber also drew, engraved, scoured, and burnished a plate of a battle. There is no mention of printing, but he did color a finished print. Undoubtedly, this was *The Georgia Militia under Gen. Floyd attacking the Creek Indians at Autossee–Novr. 29th 1813* (fig. 2). Although completed in the Reed workshop, the imprint reads 'Published by W. Phelps & Co. E. Windsor Con. March 1814.' For some unknown reason, Reed allowed a print engraved in his shop to be published under the name of his plate printer and nephew-in-law.

Another print of this period from Barber's hand, was *Commodore Perry's Victory, on Lake Erie, Over the British Fleet, commanded by Commodore Barclay, Sept. 10th 1813*. Barber noted that he drew and engraved the plate in the last week of March, and it was printed with the caption, 'Published by A. Reed & Co. E. Windsor Con. April 1814.' This print has survived in two states. One bears the initials JWB below the engraving in the right hand corner; the other is blank in that area.[22]

Although Barber became well known as a historical writer who illustrated his books with his own woodcuts, he apparently never experimented nor needed to work with this medium until well into his second year. Furthermore, there are very few notations in his diary during the years of his apprenticeship where he mentioned engraving on wood. Usually he engraved on copper.

Barber did his share of printing. He made entries, 'printed copies [certificates],' 'printing pictures with Loring,' or 'printing watch cards Huntington & Church.' Also he 'bound & trimmed [D] books,' 'bound copies,' or 'stitched and trimmed.' Miscellaneous entries such as 'Engraving watch plate Wilmington NC' or 'Counting Bills' clearly indicate that he was becoming extremely competent, and Reed now was assigning him more responsible tasks. During intervals when Barber was not engraving, he helped with rush orders. For instance, most of the month of March 1814 he colored maps that a Mr. [Markel] picked up personally on the 26th. This must have been Reed's map depicting Napoleon's retreat from Russia, a popular topic of conversation of the time.[23]

Barber's third year in the trade showed little change. That particular year he still worked in the garden at peak times, did odd jobs around the shop, and made it a point to note that he went after shad when they were running heavily in the river. Otherwise,

---

22. This engraving, illustrated in Irving S. Olds, *Bits and Pieces of American History* (New York: Privately printed, 1951), 220, lacks the initials JWB whereas a copy at the Connecticut Historical Society contains them.

23. *A Map of Europe In which are delineated the rout of the French Army, to & from Moscow, in the Campaign of 1812–That of the Campaign of 1813; and also, that of Ld. Wellington's Army in Spain*, Published by A. Reed & Co. E Windsor Con. Mar: 1814.

he continued the usual activities—engraving, drawing, scouring and burnishing plates, printing, and binding and trimming. As usual he journeyed home frequently and continued to record the arrivals and departures of visitors, workers, and the young ladies of the house.

John Warner Barber celebrated his eighteenth birthday on February 2, 1816, by sticking to his daily routine; during the evening, however, he 'Watched with Mr. Loomis.' Now he was of sufficient age to endure the morbid responsibility of sitting with a person near death. He did this several times in 1816, including twice in the Reed household. The elder Mrs. Reed died on February 8, and she was followed by Abner Reed's sister-in-law two weeks later. Two years later Barber sat with the elder Mr. Reed before he succumbed.

However, there were apparently many happy moments now. That year he attended meetings of an unknown nature, but they were probably church related as they were held at the home of a local deacon. Perhaps there was a young lady in Barber's life now, because he attended singing school through the winter of 1817 and took dancing lessons. These activities must have been a pleasant break from the daily round of chores and shop work. They also provided an escape from the confinement of a crowded household.

Responsibilities in the shop multiplied as well; in late 1815 Reed received a major commission from Barber Badger, the Boston publisher, to engrave plates for his proposed book, *The Naval Temple* (fig. 3).[24] Reed delegated to Barber the engraving on copper of at least three scenes and the frontispiece. Elkanah Tisdale (1768–1835), a Connecticut designer then living in Boston, drew the frontispiece, and Michel Felice Corné (c. 1752–1845), a marine painter known for his scenes of the War of 1812, completed the drawings for the rest of the plates.

Barber recorded in his diary that he started working on the project in December; at that time he was 'Engraving Battle of Lake

24. (Boston: Barber Badger, 1816).

Fig. 3. *The Naval Temple*. E. Tisdale inv. & del. Reed, Rawdon, Wright & Co., New York. American Antiquarian Society.

Fig. 4. *Battle of Plattsburg*. Read sc. American Antiquarian Society.

Champlain.' He did not record when he finished this plate, but he
was working on the 'Battle of Plattsburg,' on January 2, 1816, and
finished it eleven days later. On both plates the name of the engraver is misspelled 'Read' (fig. 4); and most copies lack the name
of a printer or publisher incised into the plates. However, there is
a second state of the 'Battle of Plattsburg' with the caption,
'Printed by Saml Maverick N.Y.'

   Possibly Barber was instructed to leave these plates unsigned in
order to allow Samuel Maverick (1789–1845) to fill in this information; and when adding Reed's name, Maverick simply misspelled it. Misspelling the name, Reed, was probably a common
occurrence. Daniel Burnap, Abner Reed's neighbor, made an entry in his account book for June 1791, also spelling the name
Read, and then three months later he spelled it correctly. Also
William Dunlap, in his *History of the Rise and Progress of the Arts of
Design in the United States*, spelled it Reid.[25]

   25. Hoopes, *Shop Records of Daniel Burnap*, 21; Dunlap, *History of the Rise and Progress of
the Arts of Design*, 2: 47.

Fig. 5. *Capt Sterrett in the Schr Enterprise paying tribute to Tripoli, August 1801. M. Corné*. American Antiquarian Society

This becomes comprehensible when another print in the series is examined: 'Capt Sterrett in the Schr Enterprise paying tribute to Tripoli, August 1801' (fig. 5). Barber was working on this plate on the first of May and engraved the painter's name, M. Corné, but left the rest of the acknowledgement blank. The engraving was undoubtedly finished when Badger arrived in East Windsor on May 18. No doubt he carried this plate to New York where Maverick, probably under pressure to finish the job, neglected to add the engraver's name. Barber started working on the Tisdale frontispiece May 31 and finished it June 7. This engraving has the name Reed spelled correctly, along with that of Tisdale as artist, which certainly indicates that Barber also engraved the names into the plate.

Bank note engraving accounted for a large percentage of Reed's business. Reed's grandson, Henry Reed Stiles, noted many years later that lacking modern technology 'Laborious hand work was not relieved, as at present, by curious mechanism; the old "pull" hand-press alone was used, and the printed sheets of bank-notes were sun-dried on clothes lines in the Deacon's back yard!'[26] Obviously there were many 'tricks of the trade' to acquire before one felt sufficiently competent to engrave notes difficult to counterfeit. Barber had done his homework by spending many months assisting in the preparation of plates; by the summer of 1816, the young apprentice had picked up sufficient 'tricks' to go to work on his own.

Barber devoted most of his time to bank notes throughout the rest of his apprenticeship in Reed's workshop. He frequently made entries such as 'drawing device for Hartford Bank' or 'Engraved bank plate.' Sometimes he noted the denomination, 'Engraved Mechanics 20 dol,' or 'Engraved Phenix bk NY 3 dol.' Customers included banks throughout New England, New York, and Canada. At this time, Reed was travelling extensively. Moreover, he was a member of the Connecticut House of Representatives from East Windsor in 1817 and 1818 which accounts for some of his absences.[27] Who was in charge in his absence is unknown, but there is little doubt that he had complete confidence and trust in John Warner Barber, a senior apprentice as well as an accomplished engraver.

Abner Reed's workshop must have been a place of experimentation, where tinkering was encouraged, an environment where the perfection of new technology was attempted, especially in trying to thwart counterfeiters. East Windsor had already produced two Yankees of genius, John Fitch (1743–96) and Eli Terry (1772–1852), and a case could be easily developed that Reed was the third. Fitch, an experimenter in steam-driven boats, shared a common ancestry with Reed, whose mother was a Fitch. Reed may have even known Fitch when the latter resided for a brief time in East Windsor in the mid 1790s. And Eli Terry, the first American to produce clocks in volume, was a contemporary of Reed. He was completing an apprenticeship under Daniel Burnap

26. Stiles, 2: 635.
27. See *Roll of State Officers and Members of the General Assembly of Connecticut from 1776 to 1881* (Hartford, 1881).

while Reed was down the street doing the same under Samuel May.[28]

While Fitch and Terry left their hometown, Reed returned to make his contribution. John Warner Barber, Samuel Stiles, and other young apprentices must have been part of the team that developed the technology to produce sophisticated currency difficult to counterfeit. By 1820 they had produced a complete and different set of dies for each denomination from one to ten dollars.[29] Hence a counterfeiter could not duplicate a plate and quickly change the denomination; he would have to make a separate plate for each.

By this time, Reed's notes had been examined in England, along with notes from his local competitor the Hartford Graphic Company. The British examiners found both to be '. . . decidedly superior to any engravings of the kind we have ever seen.'[30] The English were also impressed with the high quality of the paper manufactured by the Hartford firm of Hudson and Company.[31] Abner Reed was undoubtedly the driving force another Yankee genius, a master who oversaw his shop—leading Barber, Stiles, and the other apprentices in the development of new technology.

Barber also developed the habit of recording the names of individuals who worked in the shop; thus a fairly comprehensive list of these men is known today. Two boys whose names are not known followed Barber before Reed's oldest son, Abner Loring (1800–89), started in 1814. Whether he learned to engrave is unknown because Barber only mentioned his work at the press. Loring worked for Balch & Stiles in Utica and was involved with his father in East Windsor as late as 1834, when he moved with his wife to Conneaut, Ohio.[32]

Vistus Balch (1799–1884), a future engraver and portrait

---

28. For Fitch, see Stiles, 2: 263–68, and for Terry, 2: 751–52.

29. This was the claim made in a circular announcing the formation of Reed & Stiles in January 1821. A copy is at the Connecticut Historical Society.

30. *Connecticut Mirror*, February 1, 1819, 2: 3.

31. *Ibid.*

32. Stiles, 2: 639 and Barber, December 22, 1814.

draughtsman on stone, arrived February 1, 1815. According to the diary, 'Balch went home [April] 27th.' Barber did not offer any explanation for his departure, but it can be safely assumed that a conflict developed between master and employee. Yet Balch must have made friends there during his short stay and somehow learned the trade. From 1822 to 1826 he was in business in Albany, New York, with another former Reed apprentice, Ralph Rawdon, as Balch, Rawdon, and Company.

Two years later Balch and Samuel Stiles decided to take advantage of new business opportunities created by the opening of the Erie Canal. They opened a shop in Utica advertising 'Copperplate Printing neatly executed,' but the partnership lasted only a couple of years.[33] Apparently there was little business and they had difficulty getting supplies. For example, they waited weeks for a shipment of copper from Philadelphia to fulfill a map order. Help was also a problem and they were in need of a plate printer. The partners considered sending for William Phelps 'If we were sure of work to keep him in constant employ.'[34] Apparently they decided that there was insufficient work, as there was no further mention of bringing Phelps west.

They did business with the Utica Bank but ironically only with the help of their former mentor. Stiles wrote Reed on October 2, 1824, that they were asked by a Mr. Hunt, the bank's cashier, 'Can you make a copy or facsimile of one of our plates with the old die of Murray, Draper & Co?' They assured him that 'Mr. Reed had the plates to do the job.'[35] Stiles requested the needed plate and argued that Mr. Hunt's influence was crucial in securing business from other western banks. In late November Stiles wrote Reed again complaining that they had not received the plate and wrote further, 'Without the plate ... it would be a death blow to all our hopes of work from that Bank.'[36] Finally by Christmas the plate

33. A sample of their tradecard is located in SFM, 1: 102.
34. Letter from Samuel Stiles to Abner Reed, September 21, 1824, SFM, 1: 76.
35. SFM, 1: 79.
36. SFM, 1: 80.

had been sent and received; by then they had gotten more business through Balch's effort in a trip west to secure orders.

Orders, however, must have been insufficient and the logistics of doing business in a new town overwhelming. Relations between Balch and Reed were still strained even though Reed's assistance was necessary; and no doubt homesickness was a factor for Stiles. In June 1825 he returned to East Windsor and married Reed's daughter, Charlotte Sophia. Stiles returned with his bride to Utica, but by August he was already considering moving back to Hartford.[37]

After experiencing another winter in the west, Balch was ready to move to New York City. Stiles wrote to his brother that 'He [Balch] has made it [such a move] in contemplation for some time.' At the moment Stiles wanted him to remain, as business must have picked up. He wrote further, 'He does not leave here now, for the want of employment but he has more ambition for Fame than I have, and that is the only field [meaning New York City] to acquire it.'[38] The relationship between Balch and Stiles remained cordial despite the dissolution of their Utica partnership. After Stiles followed Balch to New York, they renewed their business association by opening an office on Wall Street.[39]

Samuel Stiles may have been Abner Reed's favorite apprentice, for there are engravings bearing the inscription 'Reed & Stiles sc,' from 1819, the year Stiles completed his apprenticeship. The official announcement of the partnership did not occur until 1821, when they opened a shop in rooms Reed had rented in Hartford. Also Reed might have wanted to help his future son-in-law get off to a good start. Another reason for their partnership could be that Stiles was the 'genius,' along with Reed, who made significant improvements in engraved bank notes. Whatever the reason, bank note engraving became the firm's specialty, although they continued to produce engravings for such publications as Silliman's *American Journal of Science* and woodcuts for numerous Hartford printers.

37. Robbins, 1: 1006 and SFM, 1: 86.
38. SFM, 1: 91.
39. See tradecard of Balch, Stiles & Co., SFM, 1: 104.

From Utica, Samuel Stiles moved to New York City where he settled permanently. Besides continuing an affiliation with Balch, he also formed the partnership of S. Stiles, Sherman & Smith.[40] Later he was employed with Danforth, Wright and Company until they merged with several others to form the American Bank Note Company in 1858. A year later, Stiles wrote, 'I have disconnected myself from those with whom I have so long been connected and also with the <u>great</u> Am Bk Note Company and am now about to begin life anew at the age of 63 years.'[41] That new life was with other colleagues who became disenchanted with the American Bank Note Company. These individuals formed the National Bank Note Company, and Stiles became the firm's treasurer and general clerk at an annual salary of $500.00. His new life was short-lived, however, for he died in 1861.[42]

When Stiles moved to Utica, the Hartford office was turned over to Oliver Pelton (1798–1882), another former Reed apprentice. Pelton had been working there well before the formation of Reed, Stiles & Co., for Barber visited him there in 1820.[43] After Stiles's departure, Pelton became a partner, and the firm's name changed to Reed, Stiles, Pelton & Company, although there were still accounts under the former name of the firm. By spring of 1826 Stiles complained to Reed that Pelton was not paying the bills.[44] Pelton apparently had a lifelong problem handling money. Barber recorded a year earlier, 'Lent O. Pelton 2 dols,' which he never mentioned having been repaid.[45] Later in his career while living in Boston, Pelton had financial problems with his partner, William D. Terry.[46] The problem over Pelton's management was probably the death knell of Reed, Stiles, Pelton and Company.

---

40. See circular in SFM, 1: 111.
41. SFM, 2: 140.
42. SFM, 2: 141.
43. Banknotes have survived with only the names Reed & Pelton. The Rhode Island Historical Society has several of them.
44. SFM, 1: 93.
45. Barber, September 15, 1825.
46. See 'Letters from a Bank Note Engraver to his Partner: Oliver Pelton to William D. Terry, 1834,' *Essay Proof Journal* 68 (1960): 155–62.

This firm simply went out of business; whether the company's debts were ultimately honored is unknown.

Ebenezer Fitch Reed (1799–1832), a nephew, and Frederick Bissell (1799–1870) became friends while serving their apprenticeships. In early 1821 they established Reed & Bissell in New York City, and advertised as bank note engravers and printers.[47] They also produced watch papers, but nothing else is known about their affairs.[48] In the autumn of 1824 their business was not faring well when Samuel Stiles visited them on his way to Utica. He wrote to Reed that 'I found Frederick and Eben well but with little business. . . . Frederick is dissatisfied with the business and his prospects and [I] believe determined on quitting it if he can find other employment.'[49] The business did collapse; Frederick Bissell went on to have a distinguished career as a merchant in Toledo, Ohio.[50] Ebenezer Fitch Reed stayed on in New York City and died there in 1832.[51]

John S. Horton (c. 1802–c. 1853) was a shadowy figure who joined the Reed workshop in 1815.[52] He is listed in the Providence directories of 1824, 1826, and 1828, but he was in that city as early as 1823 when he engraved the plates for *A Complete System of Stenography* by Jonathan Dodge. His advertisement, appearing in only the 1824 directory, focused on engraving and copperplate printing, but it also stated that he had a good stock of superior quality bank note paper. Sometime after 1828 he moved to Baltimore, where he is listed in that city's directories from 1837 to 1845. His name is next found in the New York City directories (1846–53) before he finally disappears.[53]

47. A sample bank note is reproduced in E. Sherry McFowble, *Two Centuries of Prints in America, 1680–1880: A Selective Catalogue of the Winterthur Museum Collection* (Charlottesville: University Press of Virginia, 1987), 502.
48. See Dorothea F. Spear, 'American Watch Papers with a Descriptive List in the American Antiquarian Society,' *Proceedings of the American Antiquarian Society*, 61 (October 1951), 349.
49. SFM, 1: 76.
50. For a biographical sketch see Stiles, 2: 90.
51. Stiles, 2: 634.
52. 'John S. Horton came.' Barber, October 23, 1815.
53. See George C. Groce and David H. Wallace, *The New-York Historical Society's Dictionary of Artists in America, 1564–1860* (New Haven: Yale University Press, 1957), 327.

Alfred Daggett (1799–1872), eventually a New Haven engraver of portraits and bank notes, arrived in East Windsor in November 1817.[54] He and Barber became friends and joined the Methodist Church together in 1821. Later in New Haven, they had shops in the same building. Daggett had the distinction of being the uncle and first teacher of John Frederick Kensett.

Lewis Fairchild (1801–80) started his apprenticeship with Asaph Willard in New Haven, but spent some time in Reed's shop before moving on to the Hartford Graphic & Bank Note Company as a draughtsman.[55] At about the same time he did some miniature painting. Fairchild worked for a brief time in the shop of Balch & Stiles in Utica before moving on to Providence and later Boston.

Reed's 'extensive and elegant engraving establishment,' as aptly described by Pease and Niles, had its share of tradesmen pass through its door. Many names are still familiar to historians of American engraving. Asahel Chapin Stiles is mentioned so often that it is logical to conclude that he and Barber became good friends. Entries such as 'Mr. Phelps got back' or 'Mr. Willard arrived' indicate that men who were a generation older returned when in need of employment.

Barber's apprenticeship, as observed through his diary, undoubtedly reflects common experience. Young men were expected to work arduously through a variety of assignments which avoided the drudgery associated with the factory system of a later era; and, at the same time, they did their share of the chores. Leisure time was granted, and participation in constructive activities was probably encouraged. Abner Reed was a strict Congregationalist and no doubt he expected his men to observe the Sabbath. Thus time was allocated from noon on Saturday to Monday morning, not only to worship but to rest and to visit family.

John Warner Barber left the Reed household after his twenty-first birthday with a letter of endorsement from his master. He

54. 'Alfred Daggett came.' Barber, November 4, 1817.
55. 'Louis Fairchild came.' Barber, June 9, 1817.

lived briefly in Hartford and permanently settled in New Haven in 1823. There he raised a family and worked for over sixty years. He became well known as a historical writer and illustrator of many books. Yet he never forgot the benevolence of his old mentor. Barber often visited Mr. and Mrs. Reed at their East Windsor home, and the elderly couple were frequent house guests of the former apprentice in New Haven over the next thirty years. No wonder that Barber commented in later years 'that he considered it a favorable circumstance that he had been a member of the family of Dea. Abner Reed, where Christian rules were adopted and where its heads felt an interest in the religious welfare of those under their charge,'[56] undoubtedly a sentiment that would have been echoed by many of the young men who passed through the workshop of Abner Reed.

56. Stiles, 2: 636.

APPRENTICES IN THE WORKSHOP OF ABNER REED

HARTFORD ERA (1803–1811)

Name	Apprenticeship	Companies	Location
William Mason (c. 1796–c. 1844)	c. 1803–1810	W. & D. H. Mason W. & A. Mason	Philadelphia
William Phelps (1785–1858)	c. 1803–1810	W. Phelps & Co.	East Windsor
Asaph Willard (1786–1880)	c. 1803–1810	Hartford Graphic Co.	Hartford Providence

EAST WINDSOR ERA (1811–1821)

Name	Apprenticeship	Companies	Location
Vistus Balch (1799–1884)	Feb. 1, 1815– Apr. 27, 1815	Balch, Rawdon & Co. V. Balch & S. Stiles Balch, Stiles & Co. Balch, Stiles, Wright & Co. Balch & Co.	Albany Utica New York New York New York
John Warner Barber (1798–1885)	Jan. 22, 1813– Sept. 1, 1819	Reed & Barber	Hartford New Haven
Frederick Bissell (1799–1870)	Apr. 22, 1816	Reed & Bissell	New York
Alfred Daggett (1799–1872)	Nov. 4, 1817	Daggett & Ely Daggett, Hinman & Co.	New Haven
Lewis Fairchild (1801–c. 1880)	June 9, 1817	Hartford Graphic Co. V. Balch & S. Stiles	Hartford Utica Providence Boston
John S. Horton	Oct. 23, 1815		Providence Baltimore New York

Name	Apprenticeship	Companies	Location
Oliver Pelton (1798–1882)	Apr. 4, 1816	Reed & Pelton	Hartford
		Reed, Stiles, Pelton & Co.	Hartford
		Terry, Pelton & Co.	Boston
Ralph Rawdon (c. 1800–c. 1877)		Balch, Rawdon & Co.	Albany
		Rawdon, Clark & Co.	Albany
		Rawdon, Wright & Co.	New York
		Rawdon, Wright & Hatch	New York
		Rawdon, Wright, Hatch & Edson	New York
		American Bank Note Co.	New York
Abner Loring Reed (1800–1889)	Dec. 22, 1814	Balch & Stiles	Utica
Ebenezer F. Reed (1799–1832)	Oct. 24, 1815	Reed & Bissell	New York
Elisha [Sill]	Mar. 20, 1813		
Asahel C. Stiles (1793–1866)	1812		
Samuel Stiles (1796–1861)	1812	Reed & Stiles	Hartford
		Reed, Stiles, Pelton & Co.	Hartford
		V. Balch & S. Stiles	Utica
		Balch, Stiles & Co.	New York
		Balch, Stiles, Wright & Co.	New York
		S. Stiles & Co.	New York
		S. Stiles, Sherman & Smith	New York
		Danforth, Wright & Co.	New York
		American Bank Note Co.	New York
		National Bank Note Co.	New York
Julius Thompson	May 5, 1813	publisher of the *Connecticut Mirror*	

˙The Lithographic Workshop, 1825–50

DAVID TATHAM

WITH THE APPEARANCE in Boston and New York in the mid-1820s of the first viable lithographic work-shops—job shops where draughtsmen drew pictorial matter to order on lithographic stone and pressmen hand-printed the images—a new means of training and nurturing artists in the United States came into being. Within a few years the medium flourished also in Philadelphia and Baltimore, and by mid-century lithographic workshops existed in nearly all of the nation's major cities. Then, in the 1850s, the part played by the workshops in the cultivation of American fine artists began to diminish rapidly as the shops themselves gave way to factory operations.[1]

The workshops of the 1820s differed from their counterparts in the older graphic arts—metal plate and wood engraving—in a number of ways, but markedly so in lithography's need for skilled

1. For histories of individual early lithographic workshops, see Georgia Brady Bumgardner, 'George and William Endicott: Commercial Lithography in New York, 1831–51,' in David Tatham, ed., *Prints and Printmakers of New York State, 1825–1940* (Syracuse: Syracuse University Press, 1986), 43–65; John Carbonell, 'Anthony Imbert, New York's Pioneer Lithographer,' in Tatham, *Prints and Printmakers*, 11–41; Bettina Norton, 'William Sharp, Accomplished Lithographer,' in *Art and Commerce: American Prints of the Nineteenth Century* (Boston: Museum of Fine Arts, 1978), 50–75; David Tatham, 'The Pendleton-Moore Shop: Lithographic Artists in Boston, 1825–1840,' *Old-Time New England* 62 (Fall 1971): 29–46; Tatham, 'John Henry Bufford, American Lithographer,' *Proceedings of the American Antiquarian Society* 86 (April 1976): 47–73. For numerous unpublished accounts of Boston lithographic shops, see the bibliography in Sally Pierce and Catharina Slautterback, *Boston Lithography, 1825–1880* (Boston: The Boston Athenæum, 1991), 183–86. My generalizations about the early shops and the instruction in drawing given in them are drawn from these sources and study of the shops' lithographs, except as otherwise noted.

DAVID TATHAM is professor of fine arts at Syracuse University.

draughtsmen capable of fluent tonal work. Because this skill was in short supply in the United States during the second quarter of the nineteenth century, the lithographic shops found it necessary to assume a teaching function. Through on-the-job instruction they developed the drawing skills of talented beginners in a direction that would serve lithographic production. Since that production hewed closely to the conventions of European academic drawing, training in a shop not only prepared a young artist for a career as a journeyman draughtsman on stone but it also gave him (or in rare cases, her) a foundation in art roughly equivalent to that offered by academies of fine art as the first stage of preparation for a career as a painter. During the thirty years between 1825 and 1855 the workshops in this way helped to launch the careers of a number of distinguished American painters, including George Loring Brown, Alfred Jacob Miller, William Rimmer, Fitz Hugh Lane, and Winslow Homer.

Little archival evidence survives to say precisely how these early shops nurtured artistic talent so well. Only fragments of their business records survive. Documentation of their equipment, quarters, and arrangements with artists is scant. We have little accurate knowledge of how many draughtsmen any shop regularly employed and how many it called on only when needed. It is easy to suppose that a draughtsman-proprietor, a pressman, a bookkeeper, and a lad-of-all-work sufficed to constitute a viable operation in the early years, with other draughtsmen on call, but some shops were clearly much larger. The questions of who taught and who learned, how often instruction took place, and in what circumstances, can be answered only with the help of conjecture. In memoirs written in old age a few artists recalled their beginnings in lithographer's shops decades earlier, and while these selective and often sentimental accounts tend to be either too brief or too prolix to answer many questions satisfactorily, they nevertheless illuminate a few things about the shops and the teaching and learning that occurred there (and we will hear from two of them below).

In some respects the best evidence of art instruction in early lithographic workshops resides in their products, the thousands of impressions of lithographic prints that enrich American graphic arts collections. To judge from the shops' prints, the quality of their instruction in the 1820s and '30s was not markedly inferior to that offered by American academies of art. The shops were, in a sense, a limited but reasonable substitute for at least the entry level of academy training, and they offered the added advantage of employment to those beginners who became proficient draughtsmen. Whether their proprietors viewed the instruction they sponsored, or at least encouraged, as anything more altruistic than a practical means of training graphic artists to meet a rapidly increasing demand for printed pictures, is another question for which no definitive answer seems possible.

The instruction itself broke from the older, simpler master/apprentice system that had prevailed among engravers of metal and wood. The importation of lithography from Europe in the 1820s put in place a new medium for which virtually no American masters then existed. The American entrepreneurs who first made a success of the medium, notably Anthony Imbert in New York and James Pendleton in Boston, turned not to graphic artists in other media (who could not in any event have helped them), but rather to painters, who already thought in tonal terms. A few of these painters, such as Rembrandt Peale and Charles Des Essarts, already knew the medium from European training, but others, such as Thomas Cole and perhaps Gherlando Marsiglia, that all-but-forgotten founding member of the National Academy of Design, probably acquired proficiency in the shops. While there is no evidence that Peale or Des Essarts or anyone else taught the first group of new recruits in the 1820s, they might have done so. Certainly their association as painters with the fledgling operations enhanced the status of the workshops.[2]

The circumstances of the early workshops militated against the

2. For Des Essarts, Cole, and Marsiglia, see Carbonell, 'Imbert,' 13–20.

traditional master/apprentice relationship so far as the teaching of skills was concerned. As often as not, the owner-proprietor possessed little or no artistic competence in the medium. Further, the expanding volume of business steadily required more trained draughtsmen than the indentured apprentice system could supply. While many promising young draughtsmen were called apprentices, and remunerated accordingly, their instruction came more often from only slightly more experienced colleagues than from any master. Teaching was a communal enterprise in which the more experienced informally taught the less experienced.

Some insight into the nature of the instruction and the aspirations of the young draughtsmen, comes from a few paragraphs in Benjamin Champney's reminiscences of his time in the Moore workshop, formerly Pendleton's, in Boston in the 1830s. Champney wrote in the 1890s, recalling events six decades earlier when, newly arrived from New Hampshire, he began his apprentice term at age seventeen.

> Here I was speedily worked in as a draughtsman for ordinary commercial work, the fine work, such as designs of figures and heads from life being done by [Robert] Cooke. F. H. Lane, afterwards well known as a marine painter, did most of the views, hotels, etc. He was very accurate in his drawing, understood perspective and naval architecture perfectly. . . . and was a good, all-round draughtsman. I was ambitious, however, and after a time got to be useful in a general way. Among others who came to try their hands at lithography was William Rimmer. . . . He was a green young man of eighteen or twenty when I first knew him, but one could see that he had great mental capacity. His drawing was always full of energy, but not suited for commercial purposes. I think he did not stay more than a year with us, but left an impression that he would one day make his mark in the world. He loved the Old Masters. . . . He must have studied engraving[s after] Michael Angelo and Greek statues to have done what he did. Perhaps he secretly studied the casts from antique work . . . for the Boston Athenæum possessed some, and the plaster workers on School Street had specimens, too. Cicci & Gary was the name of the firm, I believe. After my apprenticeship was over, I continued to work for the firm for another year . . . having taken a studio with my friend Cooke. We

worked on together [as painters] . . . hoarding the little that we made, that we might go to Europe for study. At this time there were few artists in Boston. Alvan Fisher and Thomas Doughty were painting landscapes; [Robert] Salmon, marines; and George L. Brown was exhibiting landscapes and marines. . . .

[Washington] Allston lived in Cambridge. . . . He was very gracious and encouraging in his criticism. He advised us by all means to go to Paris, thinking it the best place for study.[3]

About three years before he made this visit to Boston's most celebrated painter, Champney had spent hours at a retrospective exhibition of Allston's paintings at Harding's Gallery in Boston, and later had tagged along to listen when Allston conducted visitors through the Athenæum's collections.[4] Of the artists Champney mentions in this passage from his memoirs, it is worth noting that Brown had set an example by becoming a successful painter after beginning as a lithographer's apprentice in Boston, and that Salmon, a generation older and already well-established as a painter in Great Britain before his arrival in New England, had strengthened the connection between painting and lithography by drawing on stone in Boston and seeing his paintings copied onto stone by others.[5]

Champney's art instruction came from the Moore workshop's chief draughtsman, Cooke, who had himself been trained there not many years before and who was already transforming himself into a portrait painter. Through close observation and probably also discussion, Champney had learned as well from Lane and Rimmer, two artists of different styles, and doubtless from others also. He knew and probably copied from two- and three-dimensional works of art in Boston, listened to Allston's learned com-

3. Benjamin Champney, *Sixty Years' Memories of Art and Artists* (Woburn, Massachusetts: the author, 1900), 10–15.

4. Champney, *Memories*, 10–15.

5. Salmon's work on stone includes the lithograph *U.S. Navy Yard, Charleston, Mass.*, 1828, printed and published by Pendleton. A lithograph (by an unknown draughtsman), *Boston Harbor From Constitution Wharf*, 1842, printed by J. H. Bufford for the Naval Library and Institute, is copied from Salmon's painting of the same title. Both prints are reproduced in John Wilmerding, *Robert Salmon: Painter of Ship & Shore* (Boston: Boston Public Library, 1971), 56, 79–80.

mentaries at the Athenæum, and had the sage's encouraging send-off to lend confidence as he set out for study abroad. It is doubt-ful that the offerings of the National Academy of Design in New York or the Pennsylvania Academy of the Fine Arts in Philadel-phia around 1840 would have provided him a greatly superior ex-perience.

Champney returned from Paris to begin a long and regionally successful career as a landscape painter. The career of Charles Hart, who began in New York's Endicott shop, took a different course. Because he remained a draughtsman on stone for decades, he experienced the changes that around mid-century altered the lithographic workshop's capacity to prepare young artists for ca-reers in the fine arts. Like Champney he became an apprentice in the 1830s. In his unpublished memoirs of his years with the Endicott workshop in New York he reports that his early duties included graining stones and making lithographic crayons.[6] When he advanced to drawing on stone he also colored stock prints by hand after hours to make extra money and also, we may suppose, to learn more about color in a shop that, until the 1840s, printed only in black ink.[7]

Hart found life in the workshop much like family life, with many shared values. 'There was about the Endicott's establish-ment an artistic atmosphere. . . . There one could associate with those who, like himself, had aspirations far above commercial lithography.'[8] But there was an anxious side also that reflected how widely the young draughtsmen of the era expected to move onward and upward. He remembered that the shop's young draughtsmen feared that they might 'relinquish all . . . high artis-tic aspirations and settle down to the position of a lithographer, pure and simple, for the rest of [one's] life, and grind out com-mercial lithographs.'[9]

This is what Hart in fact did, and because of his continuing as-

6. Bumgardner, 'Endicott,' 47.
7. Ibid.
8. Ibid., 61–63.
9. Ibid., 63.

sociation with the field he was able to bring a firsthand perspective to the decline of the lithographic workshop from its status as an unplanned and improvised agency for the cultivation of artists in Jacksonian America. In its early years, he recalled, 'A lithographic artist was expected to do anything and everything. . . . The modern system of dividing work up into many branches, and each man doing one branch, is a great advantage, I think, for the establishment, but a positive injury to the operative.'[10]

The lithographic workshop as a vital place for the development of American artists began its decline at the end of the decade of the 1840s with the influx of well-trained lithographic draughtsmen and printers from Germany and France as part of the aftermath of the political unrest of 1848 in Europe. This greatly reduced the need for the workshops to train their own artists. The newly-arrived draughtsmen possessed a greater sophistication in all matters of art than did their American colleagues, whose skills now seemed, and in fact were, provincial. At the same time, art academies in the United States had at last reached a point where the best of them offered instruction in the art of drawing at a level that no workshop could match. Soon the workshop itself would be obsolete, replaced by factories in which machines would begin to supplant hand operations and specialization would narrow the aims and aspirations of those who worked on stone.

Brief as its moment of significance was, the impact on American art of the lithographic workshop of the 1820s, '30s, and '40s extended even beyond the nurturing support that it gave to individual artists. It is possible to find in the nineteenth-century painting style that we now call Luminism echoes of the common graphic style of American lithography. The artisan draughtsmen who graduated to the art of painting carried with them some of the language of drawing on stone. The meticulously modulated tonality, ambient light, apparent stillness, sharply focused middle ground—these and other qualities of Luminist American landscape painting of the 1830s and beyond surely have part of their

10. Ibid.

origins in the practice of American lithography. Transcendental-ism may have played a role in the development and acceptance of this style, as may have conventions of earlier European painting and the domesticated neoclassicism of Federal America, but the quantities of prints that issued from the lithographic workshops of the Jacksonian era trained many eyes to expect and even favor these qualities of lithography in all art. The workshops cultivated not only American artists but American taste as well.

TABLE I

AFFILIATION OF SELECTED ARTISTS WITH THE PENDLETON-MOORE SHOP, BOSTON, 1825–1840, INCLUDING SENEFELDER COMPANY AFFILIATIONS, 1828–1831

	1825	1826	1827	1828	1829	1830	1831	1832	1833	1834	1835	1836	1837	1838	1839	1840
Alexander, Francis (1800–80)	X	X	X													
Brown, George Loring (1814–89)[1]					X					X	X					
Bowen, Abel (1790–1850)	X															
Bufford, John H. (1810–70)[2]					X	X	X	X	X							
Champney, Benjamin (1817–1907)										X	X	X	X	X	X	X
Cheney, John (1801–85)[3]		X	X	X	X											
Cheney, Seth (1810–56)[4]					X	X	X	X	X							
Cooke, Robert (c. 1810–43)										X	X	X	X	X	X	X
Currier, Nathaniel (1813–88)			X	X	X	X	X	X	X							
Davis, Alexander Jackson (1803–92)[5]		X	X	X	X											
Edwards, Thomas (1795–1869)[6]	X	X	X	X	X	X	X	X								
Hoogland, William (1795–1832)	X	X	X													
Johnston, David Claypoole (1798–1865)	X	X	X	X	X	X	X	X	X	X	X	X	X	X	X	X
Kidder, James (1793–1837)					X	X										
Lane, Fitz Hugh (1804–65)								X	X	X	X	X	X	X	X	X
Nutting, Benjamin F. (1805–87)			X				X	X	X	X	X	X	X			
Penniman, John Ritto (1783–1834?)	X	X														
Peale, Rembrandt (1778–1860)			X	X												
Rimmer, William (1816–79)[7]											X	X				
Scott, John W. A. (1815–1907)							X	X	X							
Smith, John Rubens (1775–1849)		X														
Swett, Moses (1804–38)[8]	X	X	X	X	X											

1. Apprentice to Abel Bowen in wood engraving 1826–29; in London and Paris 1831–34.
2. In New York 1834–39. 3. In New York by March 1829. 4. In France by April 1833.
5. Maintained an architectural drawing business in New York throughout this period.
6. Probably affiliated with the shop later in the 1830s as well; his *Boston Directory* address for 1834 is the Pendleton shop.
7. According to Champney (*Sixty Years' Memories*, p. 11), Rimmer was at the shop for about a year. 8. In New York in 1830.

TABLE 2

BOSTON LITHOGRAPHIC PRINTING FIRMS, 1825–1850

1825 1826 1827 1828 1829 1830 1831 1832 1833 1834 1835 1836 1837 1838 1839 1840 1841 1842 1843 1844 1845 1846 1847 1848 1849 1850

Pendleton–Moore[1]

Thayer–Bufford[2]

Senefelder[3]

Jenkins & Colburn[4]

E. W. Bouve[5]

William Sharp[6]

William C. Sharp[7]

J.W.A. Scott[8]

Charles Cook

Tappan & Bradford

1. W. S. Pendleton sold to T. Moore July 30, 1836. Moore sold to Thayer in May 1840.

2. The Thayer firm became J. H. Bufford & Co. in 1844. Thayer remains listed as a lithographer at an address adjacent to Bufford until 1848 when his name does not appear in the *Boston Directory*. He reappears in 1849 as a member of Bufford and Co.

3. An outgrowth of Annin & Smith, engravers.   4. I have found no work dating from 1839.

5. In partnership with William Sharp during 1843–44.   6. Briefly in partnership with his son, Philip Sharp, with Francis Michelin, and with E. W. Bouve.   7. In partnership with his brother James C. Sharp during some of this period and later as a partner in Sharp, Pierce & Co.

8. In partnerhip with Fitz Hugh Lane as *Lane & Scott* between 1846 and 1848.

American Drawing Books and Their Impact on Fitz Hugh Lane

ELLIOT BOSTWICK DAVIS

S ELF-TAUGHT ARTIST Fitz Hugh Lane (1804–65) earned accolades during his own lifetime and, after being rediscovered during the second half of this century, is now generally acknowledged as one of the foremost American marine painters. The means and methods by which Lane—and presumably other aspiring American artists in the Northeast—taught themselves to draw, however, has not been adequately understood. The extent to which Lane's most successful marine paintings show that he was familiar with contemporary drawing practices published in drawing books is explored below. An examination of Lane's sketches and paintings suggests that he assimilated information readily available in contemporary American drawing books to develop his own unique style.

Lane's early life and artistic training in Gloucester remains uncharted territory. He was born in Gloucester in 1804 and probably attended the Gloucester district school,[1] where he may have

The author would like to thank John Wilmerding, Linda Ferber, and her husband John S. Paolella for their review of and comments on earlier drafts of this manuscript; Britt Crews, formerly curator of the Cape Ann Historical Association, for her invitation to guest curate an exhibition on Lane and American drawing books; and Colta F. Ives, formerly curator-in-charge of the Department of Prints and Illustrated Books, Metropolitan Museum of Art, for her assistance in bringing that exhibition to fruition.

1. John Wilmerding, *Fitz Hugh Lane 1804–1865. American Marine Painter* (Salem, 1964), 10. Although it is likely that Lane did attend the local common school, there is no

ELLIOT BOSTWICK DAVIS is assistant curator in the Department of Drawings and Prints at The Metropolitan Museum of Art.

initially encountered formal drawing lessons in the course of learning geometry, a skill that involved drawing the basic geometric shapes of triangles, squares, and circles and that was largely devoted to solving practical problems. At least one extant nineteenth-century geometry notebook that belonged to David Bailey, a student at the district school in the fishing community of Dunster, Massachusetts, demonstrates how geometry lessons relied upon basic drawing skills to solve practical problems. In order to determine how to sail in different winds to precise locations, Bailey painstakingly constructed various angles and triangles in his copybook.[2] Lane may have been introduced to drawing through similar lessons taught in the Gloucester school, and he may have been inspired to augment basic geometric drawing instruction with the study of fishing vessels sketched from life in and about Gloucester harbor.

Because attitudes of the residents of Cape Ann proved no exception to those held in the United States regarding a career in the fine arts, the young Lane may have felt compelled to pursue a practical avocation as a shoemaker. When he soon realized, however, that he could 'draw better than he could make shoes,'[3] he began to nurture his creative talents. The local Gloucester printer, W. E. P. Rogers, eventually recognized Lane's artistic ability, and he recommended the aspiring artist to William S. Pendleton, owner of the lithographic firm in Boston where Lane would pursue his formal training.

Eagerly embarking on his new avocation and the opportunities afforded at Pendleton's shop, Lane received his introduction to the professional art world. Unlike Philadelphia and New York, Boston did not have an academy of art until the last third of the nineteenth century; thus apprenticeships at commercial printing

---

record of his name on the school rosters preserved in the archives of the Town of Gloucester.

2. For a reproduction of one of the pages from the copybook, see Elliot Bostwick Davis, *Training the Eye and the Hand: Fitz Hugh Lane and Nineteenth-century Drawing Books*, Exh. cat. (Gloucester: Cape Ann Historical Association, 1993), Fig. 3.

3. John Wilmerding, *Lane*, 11.

Fig. 1. Robert Cooke, *Portrait of Fitz Hugh Lane*, 1835. Graphite, 8⅝ x 7⅝ in. (22 x 19.4 cm.). American Antiquarian Society.

firms functioned as important training grounds for young artists. One of his colleagues at Pendleton's, Robert Cooke (c. 1810–43), produced a highly finished pencil drawing of Lane (fig. 1)—presumably executed while the two artists visited the Gloucester coast together—and several proficient anatomical drawings now in the collection of the American Antiquarian Society. Surrounded by artists who upheld the high level of draughtsmanship practiced at Pendleton's, Lane nevertheless held his own. Recalling Lane's technical proficiency during his apprenticeship at Moore's, the successor to Pendleton's, his colleague Benjamin Champney (1817–1907) observed: 'F. H. Lane, afterwards well-known as a marine painter, did most of the views, hotels, etc. He was very accurate in his drawing, understood perspective and naval architecture perfectly, as well as the handling of the vessels, and was a good all-around draughtsman.'[4] Although Lane thrived on the comradery at the Pendleton-Moore atelier where he worked between 1833 and 1840, he would have recognized that opportunities for systematically acquiring artistic instruction were sorely lacking. If Lane wished to consult drawing books as alternative sources for learning the rudiments of an artistic education, he would have needed to glance only as far as his colleagues' easels. Many of the artists whom David Tatham traced to the Pendleton-Moore shop during Lane's tenure there created their own drawing books. For example, Thomas Edwards wrote *Juvenile Drawing Book* (1830), Benjamin F. Nutting later produced small packs of drawing cards for children that reproduced successive drawing lessons printed on a series of cards, and Rembrandt Peale wrote *Graphics*, which would later appear in at least four editions and at least fourteen printings.[5] Although John Rubens Smith did not actually work at Pendleton's, one of his drawing instruction books was produced there during the 1830s.[6]

Bolstered by his experience at a major lithographic firm, Lane was confident enough of his abilities to list himself in the *Boston*

4. Benjamin Champney, *Sixty Years' Memories of Art and Artists* (Woburn: Benjamin Champney, 1899), 10.

5. For information on the locations of the aforementioned drawing books and drawing cards, see Janice G. Schimmelman, *American Imprints on Art Through 1865: Books and Pamphlets on Drawing, Painting, Sculpture, Aesthetics, Art Criticism, and Instruction* (Boston: G. K. Hall and Co.), 1990.

6. David Tatham, 'The Pendleton-Moore Shop, Lithographic Artists in Boston, 1825–1840,' *Old-Time New England* (LXII, No. 2): 40.

Almanac of 1844 as a marine painter. Lane declared his professional status as the influence of the Hudson River School of American landscape painters exemplified by Thomas Cole (1801–48) was waning. Discouraged by his inability to attract American patrons for his ambitious, European-inspired landscape narratives, Cole expressed his disappointment with American attitudes towards the fine arts. He observed that: 'We are too young and too poor for the patronage of the Fine Arts to any extent is a common remark; but it is not a true one. We are old enough to build magnificent steam boats and decorate them with a perishable splendor that vies in costliness with the superb palaces of Europe.'[7]

Although contemporaries, Cole and Lane would later epitomize distinctly different generations of American landscape painters; nevertheless, Lane undoubtedly would have agreed with Cole's assessment of Americans' attitudes toward the fine arts. Lane, however, may have turned Americans' preoccupation with technology and their pragmatic approach to drawing to his own advantage. Cape Ann merchants appreciated Lane's accurate depictions of vessels engaged in the shipping and fishing industries that had kept their fortunes afloat, and readily patronized his ship portraits and marine scenes. Clarence Cook, who wrote a review of Lane's works in *The Independent* in 1854, observed: 'His pictures early delighted sailors for their perfect truth. Lane knows the name and place of every rope on a vessel; he knows the construction, the anatomy, the expression—and to a seaman every thing that sails has expression and individuality—he knows how she will sail under this rig, before this wind; how she looks seen stern foremost, bow foremost, to windward, to leeward, in all changes and guises; and, master of detail, he has earned his money thus far mostly painting "portraits" of vessels for sailors and owners.'[8]

7. Thomas Cole, *Lecture*, paginated in Cole's hand, 13. The New York State Library at Albany in the Archives of American Art/Smithsonian Institution, New York, Roll ALC-3.
8. Clarence Cook's article is quoted in William H. Gerdts, '"The Sea is His Home": Clarence Cook Visits Fitz Hugh Lane,' *American Art Journal* xvii, No. 3 (Summer 1985): 48–49.

In distinguishing Lane's compositions, with their distinctive horizontal design complementing balanced arrangements of sailing vessels, from those of the earlier generation of Hudson River School artists such as Cole, John Baur was the first to associate Lane with a 'luminist' style in nineteenth-century American landscape painting.[9] Scholars have since noted Lane's affinities with works by self-taught American artists sometimes known as 'folk artists,' or as I prefer to call them, limners, who learned to draw from drawing books.[10]

Lane exemplifies the claim made by John Gadsby Chapman on the frontispiece of *The American Drawing Book* (1847): 'Anyone who can learn to write can learn to draw.' Chapman's text eventually became the most popular drawing book in nineteenth-century America, where approximately 145,000 copies of drawing books were in circulation between 1820 and 1860,[11] a period that nearly spans the decades of Lane's active career. Given that 'how to' manuals for drawing were readily available, the resemblance of Lane's works to those of self-taught artists, particularly a certain conceptual approach to depicting landscape, may be attributed in part to his reliance upon drawing books. Regardless of the level of artistic instruction to which an artist aspired in nineteenth-century America, drawing books were readily accessible to professional artists, amateurs, and limners alike and undoubtedly contributed to their formation. Since Lane did not travel abroad in search of further instruction by copying the works of the great European masters—as Clarence Cook lamented in his review—drawing books undoubtedly provided him with rudimentary instruction. Limners clearly had an economic incentive to rely on drawing books. Joseph Whiting Stock (1815–55), who was active

9. For an overview of the Luminist style, see Barbara Novak, 'On Defining Luminism,' John Wilmerding, 'The Luminist Movement: Some Reflections,' and Theodore E. Stebbins, Jr., 'Luminism in Context: A New View,' John Wilmerding, ed., *American Light. The Luminist Movement 1850–1875* (Washington, D.C.: The National Gallery of Art, 1980).

10. See Barbara Novak, *American Painting of the Nineteenth Century. Realism, Idealism, and the American Experience* (New York: Harper & Row, 1979), 99–100.

11. Peter C. Marzio, *The Art Crusade. An Analysis of American Drawing Manuals, 1820–1860* (Washington, D.C.: Smithsonian Institution, 1976), 1.

during Lane's lifetime, owned Charles Davies's drawing book
Treatise on Shades and Shadows (1832), which allowed him to apply
shading to his portraits so as to command more from his clientele.[12] Similarly, drawing books could assist Lane in creating
pleasing compositions and accurate arrangements of sailing vessels on the open ocean which would appeal to his patrons who, in
turn, may have been schooled to appreciate his rendering of perspective through the methods disseminated by drawing books.

Nineteenth-century American drawing books trace their ancestry, ultimately, to the thirteenth-century medieval pattern books
of Villard d'Honnecourt. Unlike a pattern book, which provided
a repertoire of patterns for an artist or artisan to copy exactly, a
drawing book served to instruct artists in how to draw through both
illustrations and an accompanying text. During the late eighteenth
century in Britain, the popularity of drawing as a genteel pastime
encouraged amateur draughtsmen to copy from print portfolios
as the first step in learning to draw. British portfolios such as
William Austin's series of plates entitled *A Specimen of Sketching
Landscape* (1781) were accompanied by a page of introductory
text, whereas John Martin's *Character of Trees* (1817) reproduced
several plates of different species. As the demand for instruction
in landscape drawing grew during the nineteenth century, print
portfolios swelled to include more extensive written instructions,
and the forerunners of nineteenth-century American drawing
books were born. Although nineteenth-century drawing books
produced in the United States drew from Italian, French, German,
and Spanish sources, British drawing books had the greatest impact.
Like their British counterparts, the majority of American drawing
books were devoted to teaching artists how to render landscape;
moreover, the British texts which served as models for American
drawing books did not require translation; therefore the works
could be rapidly pirated and put into circulation with minimal effort on the part of American publishers and booksellers.

12. See Elliot Bostwick Davis, 'Training the Eye and the Hand: Drawing Books in
Nineteenth-Century America' (Ph.D. diss., Columbia University, 1992), 284–85.

The techniques described in British landscape drawing books were readily grafted by American artists onto a long tradition of mapmaking and surveying that had thrived in the 'New World' out of necessity. Just as Michael Baxandall considered contemporary practices of barrel gauging or mathematical games to have a significant impact on fifteenth-century painting in Italy,[13] so the appreciation of works produced by American painters and draughtsmen was conditioned in part by the value society placed on the skills of rendering vast tracts of land in perspective.[14] Early nineteenth-century educators in the United States evidently regarded surveying and rendering accurate maps as skills important to a society attempting to impose Western order upon the uncharted landscape surrounding them, and accordingly, American drawing books often included sections on surveying. Reporting on the primary-school system instituted in Maryland in the late 1820s, the *American Journal of Education* published in Boston had this to say about the importance of surveying: 'it can hardly be necessary to enlarge upon its utility. In a country so essentially agricultural as ours, where almost every man has occasion to apply in practice the principles of surveying, some general knowledge of the art is important both for his interest and convenience. He ought to understand, at least in theory, the nature and use of the compass; the measurement of land by courses and distances; and the computation of areas on the most improved methods.'[15]

The young Fitz Hugh Lane no doubt learned to improve his draughtsmanship skills by putting the techniques of mapmaking and surveying to work. Lane executed drawings out of doors in a way that essentially surveyed the landscape in small segments. In

13. Michael Baxandall, *Painting and Experience in Fifteenth-century Italy. A Primer in the Social History of Pictorial Style* (New York: Oxford University Press, 1988), 29–108. I will be further analyzing the relationship of American drawing books to the emergence of a 'period eye' evident in the landscape, figural, and perspective drawings and paintings by nineteenth-century American artists in my forthcoming book.

14. Lisa Fellows Andrus, "Measure and Design in American Painting, 1760–1860," Ph.D. diss., Columbia University, 1977, and her subsequent essay, "Design and Measurement in Liminist Art," in Wilmerding, ed., *American Light*, especially, 40.

15. *American Journal of Education*, III (Boston, 1828): 147.

a drawing of *Castine from Hospital Island* (1855) now at the Cape Ann Historical Association, he pieced together six pages from his sketchbook to create one continuous drawing.[16] He very likely drew the scene before him, taking in as large a portion of the landscape as was possible on a single sheet of paper. When it was necessary to move on to the next sheet of paper, he carefully marked with an 'X' the exact place where the sheets joined to eventually form the entire length of the designated scene. After returning to his studio, he subsequently selected which portion of the continuous harbor view he would reproduce in print, just as he indicated on a section of his drawing of Castine, 'original of my lithograph.' Lane continued to utilize such an approach in his later work when he transformed a drawing into a painting.

Although Lane experimented in his early prints and drawings with the bird's-eye vantage point favored by British drawing books for its ability to capture the terrain below, as in his lithograph *View of the Town of Gloucester* (1836) and his drawing of *Majebigweduer Narrows from North Castine* (1855),[17] his works gradually shifted away from a sweeping panorama of the landscape to more restrained horizontal compositions. Such a shift in Lane's works may have been inspired by the landscapes published in such drawing books as the text written by Fielding Lucas, Jr., and illustrated by an anonymous amateur who has been identified as Benjamin Latrobe.[18] Lucas' *Progressive Drawing Book* (1827) was largely based on the text of a British drawing book by John Varley entitled *A Treatise on the Principles of Landscape Design; with General Observations and Instructions to Young Artists* (1816–21).[19] Lucas praised Varley's work as the 'best which has yet been published in

16. For a reproduction of *Castine from Hospital Island* see Elliot Bostwick Davis, *Training the Eye and the Hand: Fitz Hugh Lane and Nineteenth-century Drawing Books*, figure 11.

17. For reproductions of both works, see Elliot Bostwick Davis, *Training the Eye and the Hand*, figures 8 and 10, respectively.

18. The identification of Benjamin Latrobe is made by John W. Foster, 'Fielding Lucas, Jr., Early 19th Century Publisher of Fine Books and Maps,' *Proceedings of the American Antiquarian Society* 65 (October 1955): 161–210.

19. Martin Hardie, *Water-colour Painting in Britain, Vol. II, The Romantic Period* (London: B. T. Batsford, Ltd., 1966), 101. For a discussion of Fielding Lucas, Jr., see Foster, 'Fielding Lucas, Jr.,' 161–211.

England'[20] and excused his reliance on Varley for the simple reason that he intended to be instructive rather than original. Landscape painters in the United States undoubtedly appreciated Lucas's adaptation of the British drawing book to an American audience; he claimed that in order for his drawing book to have an even greater interest than it would as a British reprint and to stamp it with a national character, he included sixteen hand-colored aquatints of American views taken from original sketches by Latrobe.[21]

Two of the plates from Lucas's drawing book, a view of the 'Susquehannah River Above Havre de Grace' and 'Scenery on the Hudson,' bear a striking resemblance to Lane's painting of *Bar Island and Mount Desert Mountains from Somes Settlement* (Erving and Joyce Collection, 1850).[22] In *Bar Island*, Lane envisions a sliver of foreground anchored by an upturned boat in the lower left corner, which together complement the vertical sails and hills in the scenery beyond in a manner similar to that of Lucas's depiction of the Susquehannah. The composition of Lucas's 'Scenery on the Hudson,' which leads the viewer into depth by placing a standing figure on the shore, two figures wading into the water, and vertical masts in the middle and backgrounds is also similar to the arrangement Lane created in his scene of *Stage Fort Across Gloucester Harbor* (1862, Metropolitan Museum of Art). Another plate from Lucas's drawing book, 'View on the Susquehannah' (fig. 2), depicts a solitary figure balancing a staff on his shoulders as he stands on a promontory of dark rocks with his back to us and appears to contemplate the tranquil harbor. Lane selects a similar composition for his scene of *Owl's Head, Penobscot Bay, Maine* (1862, fig. 3), in which a single figure balancing a staff also stands with his back to the viewer as he surveys the calm waters of the Maine inlet.

20. Fielding Lucas, *Lucas' Progressive Drawing Book* (Baltimore, 1827–28), 5.
21. Lucas, *Progressive Drawing Book*, vi.
22. For reproductions of illustrations from *Lucas' Progressive Drawing Book* see Elliot Bostwick Davis, *Training the Eye and the Hand*, figures 18 and 19, respectively. For an illustration of *Bar Island and Mount Desert Mountains from Somes Settlement*, see John Wilmerding, *Paintings by Fitz Hugh Lane* (Washington, D.C.: National Gallery of Art, 1988), catalogue 50.

Fig. 2. Benjamin H. B. Latrobe, 'View on the Susquehannah,' *Lucas' Progressive Drawing Book*, Plate x (Baltimore: Fielding Lucas, Jr., 1827). Etching and aquatint with hand coloring. 8¾ x 11 in. (22.2 x 29.9 cm.). Metropolitan Museum of Art, New York, Department of Drawings and Prints, Transferred from the Library, Gift of Samuel P. Avery (42.105.20).

From the second part of Lucas's drawing book I have just described, Lane may have derived inspiration for his major paintings; however, the first part of *Lucas' Progressive Drawing Book* provided artists like Lane with a systematic approach to learning how to draw landscape scenery. Lucas's drawing book featured step-by-step instructions about how to draw species of trees. Accompanying Plate Five, for example, Lucas observes: 'We do not pretend to say that the leaves of the Poplar have the figure of three shape, which we have given them in the plate; that the Pine is a collection of sharp points round a circle, or that the Oak is composed of the diamonds which we have drawn for its leaves: but these characters, when joined together, as we have joined them in the plate, produce an effect, such as remind us of the trees

Fig. 3. Fitz Hugh Lane, *Owl's Head, Penobscot Bay, Maine,* 1862. Oil on canvas. 16 x 26 in. (40.6 x 66 cm.). Museum of Fine Arts, Boston, M. and M. Karolik Collection. Courtesy, Museum of Fine Arts, Boston.

they represent.'[23] An example of a typical landscape drawing by Lane, a pencil study of a single tree in the collection of the Cape Ann Historical Association, indicates that he was working in the manner Lucas describes. One cannot be certain that Lane learned techniques of differentiating tree species in the Gloucester scenery directly from Lucas's drawing book; he may well have known such approaches to drawing foliage from numerous contemporary American drawing books reproducing instructions similar to Lucas's, including *Drawing Book of Trees* (1841) by Benjamin H. Coe (fig. 4) or William Bartholomew's *Sketches from Nature* (c. 1855). Just how prevalent these techniques were in nineteenth-century America is shown in this sketchbook belonging to a young woman, Lucy Treadwell, who carefully copied the plates of Coe's *Drawing Book of Trees* (fig. 5).

In addition to *Lucas's Progressive Drawing Book*, the most influential drawing book published in the United States during

23. Lucas, *Progressive Drawing Book*, Explanations to Plate Five.

PL. IV.

White Oak.   Beech.

Fig. 4. Benjamin H. Coe, *Drawing Book of Trees* (Hartford: E. B. and E. C. Kellogg, 1841), Plate Four. Lithograph. 6¾ x 9⅛ in. (17.2 x 23.2 cm.). The Metropolitan Museum of Art, New York, Department of Drawings and Prints, The Elisha Whittelsey Collection, The Elisha Whittelsey Fund, 1954 (54.509.11).

Lane's career was John Gadsby Chapman's *The American Drawing Book,* which first appeared serially in 1847 and was reprinted well into the 1870s. Lane undoubtedly knew Chapman's drawing book if not by way of fellow artists or by browsing through bookstalls, then most likely through the Massachusetts Charitable Mechanics' Association, which sponsored annual exhibitions of industrial products and artistic works at Fanueil Hall in Boston. A hybrid of the art pavilions of European expositions and American country fairs, the Massachusetts Charitable Mechanics' Association exhibition was an extravaganza of arts ranging from taxidermy to decoupage to the latest industrial gadget. The fine arts section of

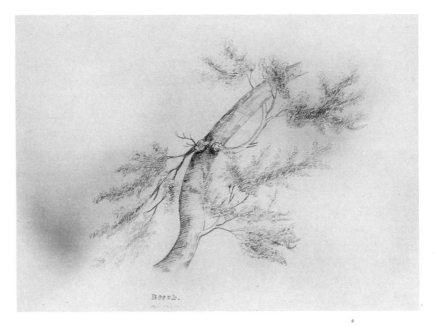

Fig. 5. Lucy Treadwell, *Sketchbook*, ca. 1844. Graphite. 9 x 11¹¹/₁₆ in. (22.8 x 29.7 cm.). American Antiquarian Society.

1847, which was found lacking in quality, displayed one of Lane's paintings along with Chapman's *The American Drawing Book* and entries ranging from lead pencils manufactured in Concord to japanned furniture from Boston. Although Lane's submissions to earlier exhibitions were favorably judged, his current work was deemed weak in aerial perspective.

The committee's emphasis upon drawing skills and improved instruction may have inspired Lane to hone his skills in rendering aerial perspective by studying a drawing book like Chapman's. Lane could have resorted to Chapman's distinct and extraordinarily efficient means of rendering perspective utilizing proportional relationships. Chapman declared that it would be easier to create the illusion of a squared pavement and define every inch of it than it would be to impose a perspectival grid on the open ocean, and yet he maintained that even marine scenes were subject to the laws of perspective.[24] There were only two constants in a marine scene—the horizon and the point of sight—from which the artist could generate proper perspective proportions. Chapman therefore instructed the artist to begin by drawing a horizontal line beneath the hull of one of the vessels and parallel to the horizon line (fig. 6). To determine the height of the vessel, a perpendicular line was then drawn from that horizontal line to the tip of the ship's mast, and being so drawn, the perpendicular established the vertical height of the ship. Having located the horizon line where the water meets the sky, the artist could fix the point of sight at any point on the horizon for the purpose of creating perspective. The artist then extended diagonal lines from the point at the top of the mast and at the base of the hull to meet the point of sight on the horizon line. The relationship of the diagonals drawn from the initial vessel and the point of sight determined a proportional scale on which the heights of the other ships floating on the calm sea could be ascertained. For example, if a ship four times the height of the initially-drawn vessel appears floating at the position indicated by the line FF in Chapman's illustration, then a perpendicular line extending from where the line FF intersects the lower diagonal to the upper diagonal will measure proportionally one length of the ship's height. To determine how tall the second ship must be to appear in proper perspective according to the vessel initially drawn, the artist then multiplied the perpendicular distance by four. The method could be repeated as many times as necessary to disperse ships of varying heights throughout the composition.

Lane's drawing of the *View in Gloucester Harbor* (fig. 7), which comprises three sheets of paper joined together, demonstrates that his method of rendering perspective indeed parallels the approach Chapman describes in *The American Drawing Book*. On the left panel of the drawing, a vessel appears on the calm water just off the rocky shore. Lane determines the height of that particular

24. John G. Chapman, *The American Drawing Book* (New York: J. S. Redfield, 1847), 144.

horizontal line through the point on which his leading figure stands, he takes the height of that figure (say six parts, or six feet), which, reduced to a scale on that line, gives all that he requires as a basis for after-operations. He must now decide upon the point of sight, which necessarily gives with it the line of the horizon, then the distance of the picture, etc. If he desires to tesselate the floor, for instance, lines drawn from the point of sight through the divisions on this horizontal line will repeat the scale as justly on the ground line and throughout the whole perspective plan of the picture as if he had begun as first suggested; the horizontal line first assumed, serving the practical purposes of a base line and with equal efficiency.

62. Again, as in the case of a view that it would be almost impracticable, if it were even necessary, to reduce to a measured perspective plan, we may select any one object which may be considered as a definite standard, and on such premises reduce all other objects and details into perfect perspective harmony, by means most simple and easy. In the case before us, it would be as difficult as unnecessary to draw a geometrical plan. It is easier to tesselate a

pavement and define every inch of it than to tesselate the traceless ocean, and yet do objects floating on its calm or disturbed surface come as equally within the government of the laws of perspective. Here we have all our lines of operation and verification to assume, except our line of the horizon and point of sight. Whichever object we select as our standard, if it be the sloop (B) nearest to us, for instance, we take its full height by a perpendicular from its vane to a central point between the water lines which mark its floating position on the perspective plane of the picture (64), and connect the extreme points of this perpendicular with the point of sight. We next decide upon the position of the ship (A) by the line F F. Supposing the ship (A) to be *three* times the height of the sloop (B), a perpendicular elevated anywhere on the line F F three times the height that the sloop would be if she were perspectively on that line (F F), will give the true height of the ship as exemplified; for it is evident that if the sloop were at the same distance as the ship (A), that is, on the line F F, her height would appear as indicated — a b — etc. Again, still more remote from us, let us suppose another ship (D) *four* times the height of the sloop, the horizontal line o o expressing that distance. By a like process do we attain the height of the ship D under such circumstances; while another ship (H), still more remote, supposed to be of the same height as A, may be thus equally, and by a similar method, brought into true

Fig. 6. John G. Chapman. *The American Drawing Book* (New York: J. S. Redfield, 1847), 144. Engraving. 12 x 9½ in. (30.5 x 24.1 cm.). The Metropolitan Museum of Art, New York, Department of Drawings and Prints, Harris Brisbane Dick Fund, 1954 (54.524.2).

Fig. 7. Fitz Hugh Lane, *View in Gloucester Harbor*, 1850s. Graphite. 9 1/2 x 34 3/4 in. (24.1 x 88.3 cm.). Cape Ann Historical Association, Gloucester, Massachusetts. Gift of Samuel H. Mansfield.

ship by creating a vertical line at the seam where the left and center panels of the drawing join. As Chapman instructs, the artist could begin to generate perspectival relationships by establishing any vertical line of known length which would then act as a constant. Consistent with Chapman's description of selecting a vertical and a point of sight, Lane draws two diagonal lines which meet the horizon line. From that triangular area in the central panel of the drawing, all the proper perspectival relationships for the scene could be generated. Lane establishes the height of the vessel he has drawn at the left by demarcating the base of the ship's hull with two horizontal lines, just as Chapman specifies.[25] Having established horizontal lines at either side of the boat's hull touching the lower diagonal, Lane draws a perpendicular line to the upper diagonal. In his *View of Gloucester Harbor*, that distance between the two diagonals is equal to the height of the vessel at the left, and Lane casts horizontal lines from the upper and lower points of the appropriate diagonal over to the left to determine the proper perspective of the sailboat. In rendering perspective, Chapman also notes that he presumes the vessels float on tranquil water in order for the proper proportional relationships to be determined accurately; Lane similarly chooses to render his vessels in the *View of Gloucester Harbor* on a becalmed inlet. With respect to the tranquil state of water, Chapman's method is indeed prac-

25. Chapman, *American Drawing Book*, 145.

Fig. 8. Fitz Hugh Lane, *Gloucester Harbor from Rocky Neck*, 1844. Oil on canvas. 29½ x 41½ in. (74.9 x 105.4 cm.). Cape Ann Historical Association, Gloucester, Massachusetts. Gift of Jane Parker Stacy in memory of George O. Stacy.

tical and efficient in establishing perspective heights without the elaborately constructed perspectival grid, which, as he observes, is impossible to create upon the surface of a vast ocean.

Several of Lane's oil paintings further suggest that the same techniques of constructing perspective underlie his finished works as well. In a work such as Lane's *Gloucester Harbor from Rocky Neck* (1844, fig. 8), which was painted before Chapman published the first edition of his drawing book, the arrangement of vessels on the water conjures up a scene of toy boats navigating a pond. By the mid-1850s, however, well after Lane may have encountered Chapman's drawing book at the Massachusetts Charitable Mechanics' Association exhibition in 1847, Lane clearly mastered the rendering of ships in perspective. Two major oils depicting *Boston Harbor at Sunset* (c. 1850–55; Museum of Fine Arts, Boston, fig. 9, and Collection of Jo Ann and Julian Ganz, Jr.), for

Fig. 9. Fitz Hugh Lane, *Boston Harbor at Sunset*, 1850–1855. Oil on canvas. 26¼ x 42 in. (66.7 x 106.7 cm.). Museum of Fine Arts, Boston, M. and M. Karolik Collection, by exchange. Courtesy, Museum of Fine Arts, Boston.

instance, derive their extraordinary symmetry and balance from Lane's ability to create an engaging arrangement of vessels on calm water. One can certainly imagine Lane constructing the relative heights of the vessels in *Boston Harbor at Sunset* (fig. 9) by casting diagonals from the height of the tallest ship down to meet the point of sight on the horizon line just as Chapman describes. In the Boston Harbor pictures as well as *Gloucester Harbor at Sunset* (late 1850s, private collection[26]), Lane disperses vessels along diagonals leading the spectator to the horizon line in a way that bears a striking formal resemblance to the illustration for Chapman's discussion of how to render perspective in a marine scene.

Chapman's discussion of perspective allows that the point of sight could be fixed arbitrarily on the horizon line. The role that the point of sight played in rendering perspective, however, was

26. For an illustration of *Gloucester Harbor at Sunset*, see Elliot Bostwick Davis, *Training the Eye and the Hand*, figure 27.

integral to the importance of training the eye through nine-teenth-century drawing instruction. Educators stressed above all that the eye was the most important of all five senses in learning and processing new information. In the *Connecticut Common School Journal* of 1842, for instance, educators claimed that students should shrug off knowledge acquired by other means and should be told that 'in order to draw correctly, he must accustom his eye to see things as they are presented to it by Nature; that is, as the infant sees them.'[27] Although Americans trusted such tools as the rule and compass to verify drawing accuracy, the majority of drawing books as exemplified by Rembrandt Peale's *Graphics* adamantly stated that the 'compasses should remain in the eye.'

Lane's drawings housed at the Cape Ann Historical Association indicate that he judged distance by eye rather than by submitting the scene before him to the rule or compass. In depicting scenes of the Gloucester Harbor and Penobscot Bay, Maine, Lane frequently oriented himself by drawing vertical lines at intervals along several sheets of paper joined together to comprise a long, panoramic view. The lines may appear as though they were measured exactly in a work such as *Camden Mountains from the South Entrance to the Harbor* (1855, Cape Ann Historical Association), however, when measured against the ruler, they are drawn at irregular intervals suggesting that the artist approximated the distances by eye. None of the extant Lane drawings at the Cape Ann Historical Association reveals traces of the compass in rendering perspective, the alternative method which Chapman described in his drawing book, but which appears to have been eschewed by Lane.

Chapman further expands his discussion of perspective to describe how an artist should depict reflections. Describing still water as a mirror of the 'real' world (fig. 10), Chapman observes: 'Fortunately in our most frequent occasions to represent reflections, they are given back by a mirror, ever most true of all other

27. *Connecticut Common School Journal*, IV, No. 4 (Hartford: February 1, 1842): 39.

but of the reality, and the way is plain. To illustrate and verify this, place a mirror level on a table, and upon it any object that first comes to hand, a book, a pen, a letter, anything—the per-

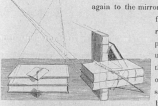

spective direction of the lines of the reflection will be found perfectly to harmonize with its original, and its image perfectly inverted. Look again to the mirror on the mantelpiece or wall, and remark how perfectly the perspective of the objects presented by it responds to the originals. Should the glass be not perpendicular, an irregularity, as it were a general upsetting of everything, will be perceived; for thus the perpendicular plane of its picture is thrown out of harmony with nature, and all its lines follow. The same would be the case if the mirror were placed flat, but not perfectly level, with regard to all objects re-

taining their horizontal and perpendicular character, but the reflected images of those resting on its surface would still harmonize with their originals, in the degree of inclination of its plane, etc.

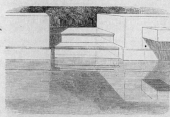

Fortunately, in our most frequent occasions to represent reflections, they are given back by a mirror, ever most true of all other objects to the level—Nature's mirror—not duplicating her perspective pictures, as presented to the eye, as if by a mere inverted tracing of their outlines, but with all the truth of an actually inverted image of the reality. Such objects as rise or occupy a position perpendicularly in reference to the mirror-like surface of the tranquil water,

preserve their real proportions. Thus, the cliff that rises in an unbroken perpendicular above its base, throws its reflection to its full height; while that of the receding hill or distant mountain,

although much higher, may scarcely be seen at all, though rising far above it—the boldness of the perpendicular cliff perspectively covering the in-

clined plane. If the point of observation could be placed exactly on a level with the water, then, and then only, would the real picture be repeated; but the slightest elevation of the point of view,

Fig. 10. John G. Chapman, *The American Drawing Book*, 167. Engraving. 12 x 9½ in. (30.5 x 24.1 cm.). The Metropolitan Museum of Art, New York, Department of Drawings and Prints, Harris Brisbane Dick Fund, 1954 (54.524.2).

objects to the level—Nature's mirror—not duplicating her perspective pictures, as presented to the eye, as if by mere inverted tracings of their outlines, but with all the truth of an actually inverted image of reality.'[28] Regarding the rendering of reflections in a marine scene, Chapman notes that if objects rise perpendicularly above the surface of the 'mirror,' which is created by the surface of the tranquil water, the shapes of the objects will preserve their real proportions.[29] Chapman is explicit that there is only one instance in which the real picture of the object's projection above the water equals the height that the object is reflected in the water; that phenomenon exists if the point of sight is exactly at the level of the water (fig. 11). For Lane to replicate Chapman's interpretation of reflections on water and to view the scene exactly at the level of the water, he would have to adopt a frog's-eye view.

Departing from methods of creating reflections described in nineteenth-century European drawing books, Chapman's discussion of reflections suggests the influence of transcendental concerns in American culture. The eye was deemed the sense most important for receiving and interpreting information about the outside world by Ralph W. Emerson, who vividly describes in his essay 'Nature' (1836) how the eye surveyed the landscape and ultimately transcended nature through vision and contemplation. He proclaims that 'The lover of nature is he whose inward and outward senses are still truly adjusted to each other.'[30] In section three of the essay devoted to 'Beauty,' Emerson observes that: 'Such is the constitution of all things, or such the plastic power of the human eye, that the primary forms, as the sky, the mountain, the tree, the animal, give us a delight in and for themselves; a pleasure arising from outline, color, motion, and grouping. This seems partly owing to the eye itself. The eye is the best of all

28. Chapman, *American Drawing Book*, 145–46.
29. Chapman, *American Drawing Book*, 148–49.
30. Ralph W. Emerson, 'Nature,' reprinted in *The Portable Emerson*, ed. Carl Bode in collaboration with Malcolm Cowley (New York: Penguin, 1981), 17.

and consequently of the line of the horizon, above the level of the water, affects the general outline of everything reflected that is not perpendicular to the water's edge, as more fully demonstrated

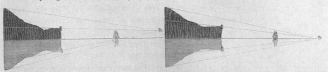

in the annexed profiles, showing the perspective relations of the various elevations. In objects
projecting over the water, as the beam in the example, the reflection will of course be naturally
longer than the receding lines of the original. An arch may repeat its outer semicircle as perfectly in its reflection as it really is, and so may be also its more receding outline, but the archway
itself is not perfectly duplicated. In the original we see less of its internal form than we do in
the reflection, for the elevation of our point of view enables us
to see farther into the reflection than within the arch itself.

Although brought to a conclusion of this chapter without
having covered, as it may seem, the whole ground of perspective, the artist-student will find therein, if not a recipe for all
his requirements, the elements and principles of the art sufficiently explained to enable him, upon their basis, to meet any
difficulty that may be presented in the course of his practical
operations. The fear of big books and elaborate treatises drive
many a one from the pursuit of knowledge, and most of all, those
devoted to the arts of design; whose restless spirits unwillingly
bear the control of any established routine; unapt to delve in
the mine of abstruse investigations, they hasten to conclusions;
and, most fortunately, all their requirements of knowledge are
progressive. Discovery and possession beget wants, and he who lives the longest, and knows the
most, has more still to learn. In the next chapter it will come in place in some degree to review
the subject of perspective as to its practical application in drawing and sketching from nature,
when an opportunity will be presented of introducing at least more generally pleasing subjects
for illustration than mere diagrams, (in which the author begs to acknowledge in advance the
assistance with which he has been favored by many of his brother-artists, as well as the productions of those of other times), that can not fail to prove acceptable.

Fig. 11. John G. Chapman, *The American Drawing Book*, 168. Engraving.
12 x 9 1/2 in. (30.5 x 24.1 cm.). The Metropolitan Museum of Art, New York,
Department of Drawings and Prints, Harris Brisbane Dick Fund, 1954
(54.524.2).

artists. By the mutual action of its structure and of the laws of light, perspective is produced, which integrates every mass of objects, of what character soever, into a well colored and shaded globe, so that where the particular objects are mean and unaffecting, the landscape which they compose is round and symmetrical.'[31]

Through his study of Chapman's *The American Drawing Book*, Lane's extraordinary compositions of the 1850s and 1860s, which have been revered by art historians for their particular qualities of balance, symmetry, and polished reflections on water that invite contemplation, give visual expression to Emerson's transcendentalism. The magic of Lane's works emanates from his ability to achieve equilibrium between his depictions of nature based on drawings rendered out-of-doors in front of the 'real' scene and his vision of the scene as he imagined it in his mind's eye, suspended in time. Although his seascapes seem at first glance to represent the Gloucester scenery with a high degree of verisimilitude, his awareness of Chapman's *American Drawing Book* may have inspired him to render the world around him in a particularly idealized way. In the *Western Shore with Norman's Woe* (fig. 12) reflections in the water are handled so masterfully that the viewer is confronted with an image that evokes both contemplation and disorientation of where the real land leaves off and the illusion of its reflection begins. By selecting a gently angled slice of the curved inlet at the Western Shore, Lane encourages the viewer to enter the composition at the lower left corner and to follow the inclined shore around to a diminishing spit of land leading back out to the horizon. Lane's viewpoint allows the spit of land to join the water's edge precisely at the horizon and to effectively extend the horizontal formed by the shore to the shape of the small island of Norman's Woe, which floats just off the coast. Above the gleaming surface of the calm water, the land swell of Norman's Woe assumes an abstract, two-dimensional shape, which appears to be gradually whittled down to a fine point. Lane may have ex-

31. Ralph W. Emerson, 'Nature,' 13–14.

Fig. 12. Fitz Hugh Lane, *The Western Shore with Norman's Woe*, 1862. Oil on canvas. 21¹/₂ x 34¹/₄ in (54.6 x 89.5 cm.). Cape Ann Historical Association, Gloucester, Massachusetts. Gift of Isabel B. Lane.

ecuted his drawings of the Gloucester coast in a small skiff, which would have placed his eye nearly at the water's level, yet his creative choice in selecting the point of sight at the level of the water nonetheless remains consistent with both Chapman's instructions and the image he envisioned in his mind's eye.

Other American artists would also take up the rendering of reflections in which the height that the land rises above the water is exactly equal to the reflection of the land in the water. John F. Kensett depicts such reflections in his view of *The Shrewsbury River* (1859, The New-York Historical Society), and Thomas Eakins creates similar reflections in his view of *Max Schmidt in a Single Skull* (1871, The Metropolitan Museum of Art). Winslow Homer would later experiment with rendering the frog's-eye view in his watercolor, *The Mink Pond* (1891, Fogg Art Museum).

Just as Emerson began with the empirical facts of nature and worked toward the spiritual through contemplation, so Lane's viewpoint, placed at exactly the level of the water, balances in a perfect and timeless state an image of the real world based on his knowledge of topographical drawing and an image of the ideal world inspired by Chapman's discussion of rendering perspective. As Clarence Cook observed of the artist in 1854: 'The man who can comparatively late in life take up a new art, and without masters, without models, without great encouragement from without, can reach in fifteen years the point which Lane has attained, has true genius, and will make men acknowledge it. He has reached the point by patient hard labor, by the simple but severe method which genius always uses, and always used.'[32] And, as one might add to Cook's assessment, Lane reached that pinnacle of visual expression with a little help from nineteenth-century drawing books.

32. Gerdts, 'The Sea is His Home,' 49.

The Plan Book Drawings of the New Orleans Notarial Archives: Legal Background and Artistic Development

SALLY K. REEVES

T HE NEW ORLEANS Notarial Archives was created by an act of the Louisiana State Legislature in 1867. It is the only notarial archives in the United States, Louisiana being the nation's only civil law (as opposed to common law) state. The Archives bears similarities to those repositories of notarial records found in other civil law jurisdictions such as Quebec, Mexico, France, or Spain. The following article traces the origin and development of this unusual genre of architectural and topographical drawings, and explains their context within the civil law notarial system of New Orleans.

Notarial acts in civil law jurisdictions are in essence contracts between living people or officially recorded declarations by individuals. In New Orleans, these contracts include sales of real property or of slaves, mortgages, leases, building and marriage contracts, wills, procurations, emancipations, business incorporations, family meetings, meetings of creditors, and so on. There are also numerous maritime documents, including captains' protests after mishaps at sea, sales of every kind of vessel, 'bottomry' bonds, and charter parties. The office holds the records of some 6,000 Orleans

SALLY K. REEVES is archivist in the Notarial Archives in New Orleans. This paper was presented at the semiannual meeting of the American Antiquarian Society at The Arsenal on April 22, 1995.

Parish notaries whose acts date from 1731 to the present. The total holdings consist of over 37,000 volumes containing about 35,000,000 pages of original textual and visual materials (c. 26,500 linear feet). The office continues to grow, having received over 58,000 new acts and bound over 400 books last year (1994).

The collection includes approximately 240,000 pages of colonial period (pre-1803) records. New Orleans was founded on behalf of the French government and the Company of the Indies by the Canadian explorer and military officer Jean Baptiste LeMoyne de Bienville in 1718. Forty-five years later, following the defeat of the French in Canada in the Seven Years' War, the French king donated the Louisiana colony to his Spanish Bourbon cousin. The Spanish effectively governed the colony from 1768 until 1803, when they gave it back to France, and twenty days later, Napoleon sold Louisiana to the United States.

Records in the Notarial Archives from the French period date from 1731 to 1768 and are scattered, limited to about 7,000 pages. Still, they include sales of property and slaves, procurations, petitions, leases, inventories of estate, and some wills and marriage contracts, all of which illuminate daily life in this elusive period. Spanish period documents date from 1768 to 1803, and amount to about 235,000 pages with every kind of act. Nineteenth-century volumes amount to about 4,500,000 pages of which roughly a third are in French. Nearly all of the rest of the acts are in English, with a smattering in German and Italian.

DESCRIPTION AND UNDERLYING VALUES OF
CIVIL LAW NOTARIAL PRACTICE

The civil law notary is a highly trained professional who transcribes into documentary language the agreements or individual declarations of parties who appear before him. The notary then functions as an archivist of the document he creates. The notary is a semipublic official whose signature to a document guarantees the identity of appearing parties, along with the authenticity of their agreements and the genuineness of their signatures. Unlike the modern attorney representing the interests of one side in a transaction, the traditional notary is a disinterested third party who represents both sides. He makes sure that the contracts he witnesses are neither onerous (unfair to one side) nor vague, which would make them subject to litigation later. In doing so, he uses a generous amount of what today we might consider 'boiler plate,' but which the French called 'les formulaires'—stock phrases that really represent the wisdom of centuries distilled into a formula. In trying to ensure that acts were flawless and thus not prone to be litigated later, the law set itself up as a benign influence that promoted stability in society, championed the family, and provided a secure and inexpensive framework for citizens to conduct their private business. They used the notarial act to ascertain and give permanent evidence to their rights. They could count on that evidence because the act bears on its face all that is needed for a legal contract. It also gives evidence to the accidents of its preservation, in that it falls chronologically in the notarial book which has been subject continuously to public scrutiny. Thus private law could proceed without the intervention of 'meddling lawyers.' Indeed, the notarial system tended to obviate the need for numerous lawyers in the colony, and militated against the litigious society.

There was litigation, of course, but it is not reflected in notarial acts. The Archives is in the courthouse, but does not function to preserve adversarial-style court proceedings. Notarial acts involving more than one party are invariably amicable agreements. They represent what functions in society, not what malfunctions.

Notarial acts also generally reflect relationships between private parties, not between the individual and the state. For this reason, the Archives does not hold permits, licenses, or other records that show a hierarchical relationship between parties. If the state appeared in a notarial record, it would be as a contracting, thus equal, party to the act.

THE NOTARY AS ARCHIVIST

By law, the notary had a serious obligation to preserve his acts indefinitely. As a precaution against fire, he had to locate his *étude* or office in a brick building with a tile roof. He had to bind and conserve his acts and plans in chronological order within pre-scribed intervals and make them available for public inspection during regular hours. He also had exclusive right to make 'true' or authenticated copies from his acts, the intellectual concept for which derives from medieval times.

Before 1867 the New Orleans notary achieved a certain per-manence by officially passing his records down to a commissioned successor in office. After 1867, Louisiana law provided for the Notarial Archives to function as the preserving agent, authorizing the custodian to demand and retain the complete works of de-ceased or retired notaries. Over the years the various safeguards in the system provided for the survival of the collection that exists today in spite of war, political change, and Louisiana's damp, in-sect-infested, flood- and hurricane-prone environment.

DESCRIPTION OF THE PLAN BOOK COLLECTION

Perhaps the most treasured documents that the notaries pre-served were the watercolor surveys kept in their Plan Books. Some 5,200 of these oversized, 'engineer's scale' (approximately 1 inch to 23 feet) nineteenth-century architectural drawings and plot plans have survived in the collection. The collection itself dates from 1803 to 1918, with seventy percent of the drawings falling between 1830 and 1860. Individual drawings average just over 38 inches long by something over 24 [.27] inches wide. A few are as small as 1.5 by 2 feet, and a number are in the range of 10 feet by 6 feet. The largest is over 25 feet long and 5 feet wide. The drawings were signed and dated by trained civil engineers and surveyors and an occasional architect. They are the visual prod-ucts of lot surveys, usually drawn to scale and measured down to the 'line,' an eighth part of an inch. The drawing grounds were frequently rendered in heavy watercolors, hues of light or deep pink, bright blues, yellows, corals, and greens. The buildings illustrated were painted and detailed in an attempt to show exact sizes, shapes, materials, colors, siting, and floor plan or roof massing.

This attempt at authenticity was a function of the drawings' provenance. They were usually created for public notice, to advertise judicially-ordered sales. The notice attracted bidders to ensure that properties sold at fair market value, which would—in accordance with the underlying principles of civil law—promote the stability of society by protecting the rights of multiple owners, women, minors, heirs, or creditors.

A week or so after the winning bidders were 'adjudicated' at the auction, the buyer and seller executed an authentic act of sale at a specified notary's office. At that time the notary took the plan used to advertise the sale and 'deposited it in his office,' to make it part of his permanent archives. Sometimes he also signed and dated or *paraphed* it to identify the visual material with the corresponding act. He did all of this to provide permanent tangible proof that the properties had been duly advertised before being sold; to clarify title; and because the rules of civil procedure mandated that both the buyer and the seller were bound by what had been advertised. There was an old formulary in French acts that always stated after the property description that the buyer had *vu et visité la proprieté à son loisir*, in other words, had viewed and visited the property at his leisure and therefore needed no further description. The realistic drawings, displayed over the course of weeks at public gathering places, provided a way to view the property at leisure in a busy world. But their subsequent filing in the notary's plan books converted the documents into contractual evidence.

The oversized 'Plan Books' continued to be preserved in the notarial *études* until the Notarial Archives was founded in 1867 or until the late nineteenth-century notaries died or retired. As a result of these historical events, the Notarial Archives has a collection the likes of which we have searched in vain to find a duplicate. Why did the custom of making drawings such as this grow up in New Orleans during the nineteenth century and not elsewhere? The answer seems to lie in our civil law background, where clues to the evolution of third-party notice have been around since legal scholars first began to study and analyze Louisiana's colonial records during the early twentieth century.[1]

It seems that the notion of giving third-party notice before a sale came to Louisiana with the French at the turn of the eighteenth century. At that time the founders were heir to a legal system that drew partly on written Roman law as codified by Justinian in the sixth century and filtered through medieval times to central Europe and partly on Germanic custom. During the seventeenth century the great French jurist Jean Domat began to systematize and unify Roman rules, royal ordinances, and Frankish customs as they applied in France, and he was followed during the eighteenth century by Robert Pothier, who contributed to the development of civil procedure.[2] By 1731, when the French Colonial period holdings begin at the Archives, documents show that the notion of third-party notice was so regularized and well developed that one suspects it either had been evolving for a long time, or was based on an exact ordinance that was itself a product of systematized law. In order to sell property in New Orleans, an eighteenth-century land or slave owner had to apply to the *commissionaire ordonnateur* of the Superior Council for permission. That permission had to be in writing, and the signed and dated document had to be attached to the act of sale. And if the *ordonnateur* did give permission, it was generally conditioned on 'observing the usual formalities.' Only rarely, because of some special waiver, was permission granted without the formalities.[3]

1. See, for example, Henry Plauché Dart, 'A Judicial Auction Sale in Louisiana, 1739,' *Louisiana Historical Quarterly* 8:3 (July 1925), 382–88.

2. A. N. Yiannopoulos, *Louisiana Civil Law System Coursebook, Part 1* (Baton Rouge, La., 1977), 18.

3. For example, sale of property, Meunier to Lefevre, Henri, notary, January 19, 1738. French series 2:9273–76.

One wonders if this was an overly paternalistic society. What business was it of the *ordonnateur* that a property owner, even in a colony, should want to sell his house or his lot? Did the government really need to control the people's business at such a level? It seems that only in analyzing the 'usual formalities' part can we put these questions into a better historical perspective. The permits and formalities were functioning as a property registration and third-party notice system. In the absence of a recordation office, these would protect other landowners if the seller did not have true title. They would also uncover any debts he might owe on it. If a landowner's property was mortgaged, he could still sell it, but the encumbrance had to go with it.

The 'usual formalities' consisted in having the *greffier*, a court official, provide for an elaborate public notice procedure which he conducted in a precise manner. On three consecutive Sundays, he would post a notice of the sale on the outside of the church door at the hour of high Mass, the one time of the week that everyone could be expected to be in town. In the case of New Orleans, this was the church of St. Louis located on the public square, now Jackson Square. The notice was also posted on the door of the Council, this also being in a building on the square. After posting the notice—what the French called the *affiche*, still the French word for poster—the notary and court officials would wait 'at the bar of the court' on Wednesday from ten a.m. until the candle burned down to a precise level. Anyone who wanted to bid on the property could appear at the office, make his bid, or make opposition to the sale. If someone wanted to cover the bid, he could. This procedure was repeated on three consecutive Sundays of posting followed by three consecutive Wednesdays of receiving. A march through town with the beating of the drums announcing the sale accompanied the program. At the end of the whole process, the *dernier enrichisseur,* or last and final bidder, was the winner. We might note here that a few of those auctions featured some spirited bidding that upped the price significantly.[4]

4. For example, sale Rixner to Petit, April 28, 1762, French series 2:67126–38.

The *proces-verbal*, or written description of oral proceedings, one of the customary attachments to the notarial act, documents the steps taken at the auction. The practice of attaching the *proces-verbal* to acts continued throughout the nineteenth century.

It was from the custom of the *affiche* that the genre of notarial plan book drawings grew in New Orleans. After the onset of American domination in 1803, New Orleans society became more heterogeneous, while at the same time the economy boomed. As the Catholic Church declined as the center of the urban universe, coffee houses, hotels, and merchant exchanges began to take their place as the city's social centers. A new, weekday, commercial venue paved the way for notices more elaborate than the old *affiches* once posted at Sunday Mass. During this period too, European-trained civil engineers from places like the *Ecole Polytechnique* and the *Ecole des Ponts et Chaussées* began to appear in New Orleans in increasing numbers, some as war refugees. These former military engineers were capable of making professional plans and surveys of a type that would serve the city's growing land-based commerce.

One of the earliest and most well known of these surveyors was Barthelemy Lafon, a Frenchman who arrived in New Orleans in 1790 and worked there until his death in 1820.[5] Lafon designed buildings, surveyed both city and plantation lands as deputy surveyor for the state, laid out towns and *faubourgs*, speculated in land, and dabbled in theater and privateering. His classic French drawing style was spiced with a certain flourish that can be recognized in a moment.

Lafon trained as a civil engineer, one of New Orleans's great early city surveyors, Joseph Pilié, teaching him 'geography, copying, and redrawing . . . plans, maps and drawings.'[6] Pilié was a pioneer in the creation of the archival drawing collection. Born in Mirabilis, Ste. Domingue, in 1789, he came to New Orleans as a

5. *Historic New Orleans Collection Quarterly* XI:1 (Winter 1993), 10–11.
6. Barthelemy Lafon Contract Book, February 17, 1805 (Mss. #316, Historic New Orleans Collection).

child with his family, escaping the slave rebellion of the 1790s. He apprenticed with Lafon, began making surveys in 1807, taught art and made scenic designs for a decade, and became city surveyor in 1819.[7] He continued to work as a surveyor either for the city or independently until his death in 1846. Between the Public Library and the Notarial Archives, 327 of Pilié's plans have been catalogued to date—228 of these at the Archives, and more being found all the time.

In all of the *richesse* of Pilié's work, we have few building elevations by him, but notably an 1826 design for the Mariners' Church on Canal Street. He is also credited with the design of Oak Alley Plantation in St. James Parish, built by his wife's relatives during the early 1830s. Pilié's real importance, however, lies in the day-to-day work he did as city surveyor. In the Archives are his drawings for the city's new powder magazine, for a major new levee, for wharves, the French Market, and the St. Mary Market. He laid out lot lines, wrote specifications for city contracts, designed a huge prison, built little bridges, and certified boundaries. His style reflected classic French conservatism=modestly-scaled plans of two to three feet with precise black Roman lettering, soft pink backgrounds, and lots of ground washed in a pale yellow.

About 1819 Pilié seems to have introduced in the city the *indication*, a precisely-articulated roof shape on a topographical plan. The *indication* looks like a monopoly house. While it does not display a façade, it does indicate the building's footprint, and gives us a precise idea of siting, scale, and roof massing. Combined with what we know about New Orleans architecture from this early-nineteenth-century period, we can surmise other details from these drawings. Numerous other surveyors would follow Pilié's lead in providing *indications* for topographical drawings during the following two decades.

In 1823 Pilié also made an important early plan of a complex in downtown New Orleans, providing both elevations and indica-

7. John H. Mahe II and Roseanne McCaffery, *Encyclopedia of New Orleans Artists, 1718–1918*, The Historic New Orleans Collection, n.p [New Orleans], 1987, 306–7.

tions of the houses, kitchens, and warehouses on the site. Like
other archival drawings in the Plan Book collection, this was not
a design drawing, not a drawing *for* a building complex, but a
drawing *of* a building complex. It was made for an auction, for
public notice. Simple as it is, with little façade detail and drawn in
the classic school of architectural drawings whose chief aim is to
show the effect of light and shadow on building forms, the drawing nevertheless constitutes an important link between the topographical drawing without elevation and the glorious pictorial ex-
ercises that were to follow in the 1830s (fig. 1).

With a few exceptions such as the preceding, Joseph Pilié did
not reach very far beyond the *indication* in his daily work. But he
led the way for others, notably his son Louis H. Pilié, who followed the father as city surveyor and had a long career of his own.
Louis H. would live through the coming of age of the Plan Book
drawings as a unique genre in New Orleans. In his time, the city
filled with talented engineers and surveyors who showed in their
drawings not only competence with line and color, but also an obvious love for the objects of their representations.

A good example of the well-developed drawing is found in Plan
Book 48, Folio 2. 'PLAN / OF THREE PROPERTIES / THIRD DISTR.'
SIGNED: 'New Orleans February 25th 1860 / E. Surgi & A. Persac
/ Civil Engineers / 130 Exchange Alley' (watercolor, ink on paper,
49½' x 24½') (fig. 2).

This drawing contains two separate building elevations, one at
the top and another at the bottom. They show three Creole cottages for sale on Frenchmen and Casa Calvo Streets, backed by
Peace and Moreau. The top elevation depicts a four-bay Creole
cottage with a high, hipped roof and two dormers. Each shuttered
opening has a fanlight transom. A sign hanging over the door tells
us that the building is Henri's shop. Architectural details such as
the transom designs, the brick sawtooth row, and the wrought-
iron supports under the overhang suggest that the cottage was
probably built during the late 1820s.

At the bottom of the plan is a second elevation of two four-bay,

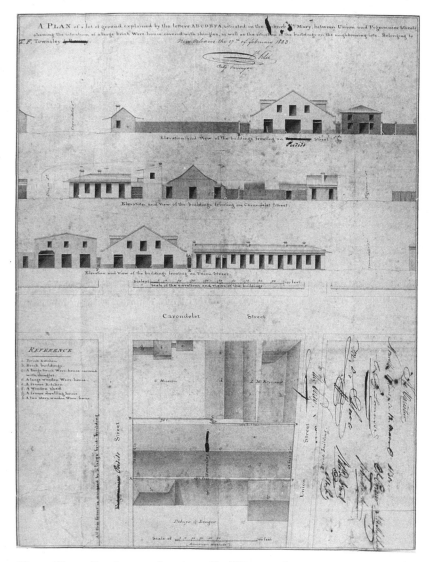

Fig. 1. The earliest known elevation of buildings made to accompany an auction sale in New Orleans showing the early, restrained style of Joseph Pilié, City Surveyor. 'Plan of a lot of ground explained by the letters ABCDEFA . . . showing the situation of a large brick ware-house covered with shingles, as well as the situation of the buildings on the neighboring lots. . . .' / New Orleans the 17th of February 1823 / Jh Pilié / City Surveyor. (Plan attached to act before Felix de Armes, notary, March 12, 1830.) Courtesy, Custodian of Notarial Records, New Orleans, La.

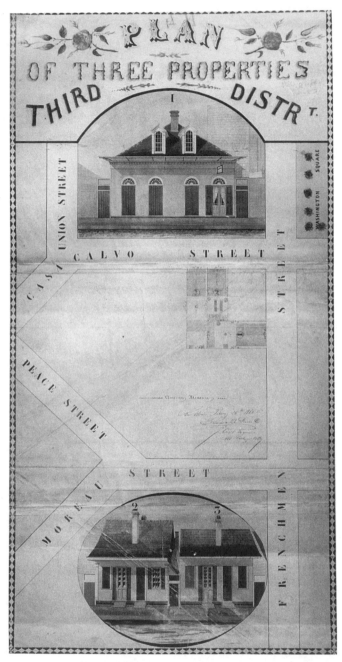

Fig. 2. Plans and elevations of three Creole cottages in the Faubourg Marigny showing the artistic accomplishments of the artist M. Adrien Persac, collaborating with Surgi, the civil engineer. 'Plan of Three Properties / Third Distr' [signed] 'New Orleans February 25th 1863 / E. Surgi and A. Persac /Civil Engineers / 130 Exchange Alley.' Plan Book 48, folio 2, New Orleans Notarial Archives. Courtesy of Notarial Records, New Orleans, La.

gable-sided Creole cottages, less distinguished than the first house. The cottage on lot 3 is the smallest and simplest of the group, and has little façade detail. It probably dates to the 1820s. Lot 2's cottage, judging from the overhang design and pilasters, probably dates to the 1830s.

The site plan in the middle of the drawing shows us that the first house (on lot 1) faces Frenchmen Street in the Faubourg Marigny, an early suburb just downriver from the Vieux Carré. Behind it is a two-story kitchen, along with privies, cistern, a well, and a shed. The smaller houses on lots 2 and 3 face Casa Calvo (now Royal) Street, and have their own kitchens, cisterns, and so on. It should be noted that in all three main house floor plans halls are lacking. This feature is one of the chief characteristics of the early Creole cottage, which typically has four main rooms with interior chimneys, and two rear *cabinets* (small rooms) flanking a recessed *cabinet* gallery. This is a decidedly Creole floor plan, one that contrasts sharply with the side-hall floor plans of American or Anglo designs found in predominantly Anglo neighborhoods and cities.

The collection is full of contrasts between French and American architectural types and styles—stair shapes and locations, roof shapes and visibility, halls and the lack of halls, formal (French) and romantic (Anglo) garden plans; showy (Anglo) and simple (French) entrances, or the location of entrances, front (Anglo) and rear (French). Creoles entered their homes through *porte-cocheres*, 'dog-trots,' exterior side alleys, and interior side alleys. All of these features can be found on various floor plans depicted in the collection.

CIVIL ENGINEERS, SURVEYORS, AND ARTISTS

Eugene Surgi and Adrien Persac, who signed this plan February 25, 1860, were two of the most important creators in this collection. Surgi, a Parisian whose brother Louis was a military engineer for Napoleon, came to New Orleans during the 1830s and with Louis spent a career making plans and industrial designs.

Eugene Surgi would have done the survey work for the lot lines and building dimensions in the sample drawing. His collaborator Persac, on the other hand, was an artist and would have painted the pictures.

Marie Adrien Persac was one of the most accomplished artists represented in the collection. Born in Lyons about 1823, he was active in the New Orleans area as a painter, lithographer, and art teacher from 1857 to 1872. He is best known for his idyllic plantation scenes, and has been described as 'a master of watercolor technique' with great skill in detailing. Persac is respected as an artist in Europe as well as in New Orleans. The Historic New Orleans Collection some years ago purchased from a London dealer a splendid watercolor view of New Orleans's riverfront in 1858, considered Persac's earliest extant work.[8] It had hung in an office in Paris for many years. The Louvre also has some Persac paintings. The Notarial Archives has thirty-three large Persac drawings. Their distinctive features include masterful detail, complex hues, a sense of lighting, depth, and atmosphere, human figures drawn in to enhance street scenes, and well-labeled floor plans.

Two other surveyor-artists of note in the collection are Pietro Gualdi and Charles de Armas. Gualdi was born in Capri, Italy, in 1808, and died in New Orleans in 1857. He treated his drawings like operatic stage settings, with a sense of drama in the immediacy of the composition and with figures added both for scale and for theatrical effect. Clouds float in the skies—hardly needed to document a property. Shadow lines, which the draftsman would use to indicate depth in brick or framework details, become in the Gualdi drawings indicators of time of day or suggestions of relief from the heat. Charles Arthur de Armas was a Creole born in New Orleans in 1824 to a long line of notaries. He was a French classicist who, like Joseph Pilié, preferred control to drama in his drawings. His works are more linear than painterly, his palette limited, almost subdued. The Archives has 275 of his plans dating

8. *The Historic New Orleans Collection Newsletter*, Vol. VI, No. 4 (Fall 1988).

between July 1848 and December 1867, after which his brother Arthur de Armas completed many more in the same distinctive style, working until 1887. With Persac and Hedin, mentioned below, Charles de Armas may be considered among the top three practitioners represented in the collection. Both de Armas and Gualdi were trained in perspective and capable of creating 'single view' drawings in which the front plane is drawn at an angle to the paper, allowing the viewer to see three dimensions, including the front, a side, and the roof. This is in distinction to the 'orthographic' or right-angle drawing, meaning that the planes of the object depicted are parallel to the bottom and sides of the page, so that one generally sees the front only or the side only.

Graphically speaking, many of the drawings should be described as 'orthographic topographical elevations,' that is, right angle, front plane depictions of buildings already built. As the title portions state, they are plans *of* properties with buildings, not plans *for* properties with buildings. With very few exceptions, these are not design drawings. They show properties after they had been owned and lived in for a generation or two, and the people had died or lost out to creditors. Sometimes, however, they depict speculatively-built cottages such as a row developed on Esplanade Avenue in the 1840s. In this case, the drawing was made for marketing the development and the auction sale was entirely elective. We are still not looking at a design drawing, however. The office does have this type of document, but in the building contract collection.

Persac, Gualdi, and de Armas were only three of many artists who painted the plans and elevations in the collection. We have identified over 133 different signatures on the plans between 1803 and 1918, including that of a free man of color, Norbert Rillieux. The Prussian-born engineer Charles F. Zimpel, known for his fine map making and line drawings, is represented in quite a few plans of the 1830s. Another frequently-found European is Benjamin Buisson (1793–1874), who attended L'École Polytechnique in Paris and became a military engineer in the army of

Napoleon at a tender age, sought a new life in New Orleans after Waterloo, and enjoyed a long and successful second career here as a civil rather than a military engineer. There are several other possibly German representatives with names such as Moellhausen, Engelhardt, Egloffstein, and Schlarbaum. There was a John Schreiber, an Adolph Knell, Cuno Werner, and Ludwig Reizenstein, believed to be the person of that name who became a great innovator in the science of lithography. Some of them seem to have influenced the others to adapt a more painterly style towards mid-century.

It was the Teutonic-sounding Henry Moellhausen, it seems, along with Louis Surgi, who began to escalate the competition during the 1840s and push the genre of drawings to new heights of attractiveness. Moellhausen's plans, with their startling German Gothic and colorful Tuscan title lettering, were perhaps the first to break out of the classic mold followed so stringently by Pilié, de Armas, Zimpel, Allou d'Hemecourt, and others. Not always a great renderer, Moellhausen was adept at making the *toute ensemble* of a drawing attractive to the eye, even if the house it had to sell was of modest value or indeed if there was only a bare lot to sell. Moellhausen and Surgi used a variety of title colors during the 1840s and went beyond the convention of pink and yellow to render backgrounds (fig. 3). Moellhausen was the first to supply little area maps to his drawings, giving the product a readable setting and supplying information about neighborhood amenities. Surgi seems to have pioneered the technique of the *entourage* within the genre, adding engaging little figures like those on the Esplanade Avenue row to his drawings, and generally making them more charming than sober, rather unlike the works of Pilié.

Both Surgi and Moellhausen pointed the way to the work of Carl Axel Hedin, a Stockholm-born artist whose work makes the biggest impact on viewers. We know little of his personal life other than that he was born in 1810 and died in 1858. The Archives has 547 drawings either by his hand or out of his shop dating between January 1846 and May 1866.

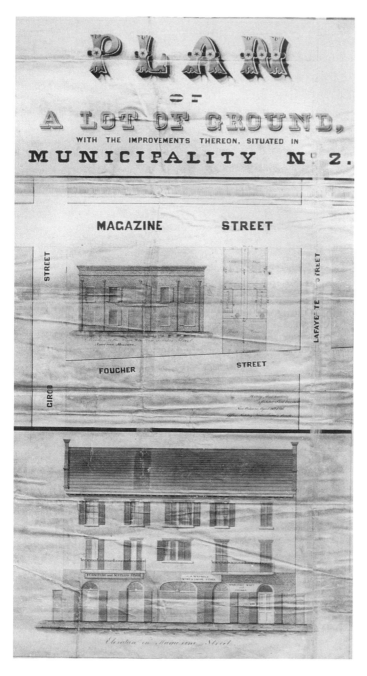

Fig. 3. Elevation by Henry Moellhausen showing the attractive graphic style of title lettering of which he was a leading proponent during the 1840s. [signed] 'Henry Mollhausen / Architect and Civil Engineer / New Orleans April 20th 1846.' Plan Book 25, folio 11, New Orleans Notarial Archives. Courtesy, Custodian of Notarial Records, New Orleans, La.

It was Hedin, perhaps, who brought the genre of civil engineers' plans in New Orleans to its greatest height. While he generally eschewed the single view drawing and ignored or was ignorant of perspective, he developed his orthographic views to their highest potential. Some of his drawings are nothing short of spectacular—tours de force of color, composition, and line. If their purpose was to get and hold the attention of businessmen and shoppers in a crowded, loud hotel rotunda or mercantile exchange, surely they must have succeeded. Hedin used the technique of scale quite effectively to make his points, combining this with an intensity of color and a beauty of form that almost 150 years later can still take one's breath away. His titles alone are an exercise in graphic art, with complex Tuscan-style letters over lines of multicolored Gothic, Clarendon, and Roman (fig. 4). His backgrounds, constructed from a patented azure blue contrasting with intense pinks and yellows, envelop noble buildings of bright red brick or gleaming white wood set in gardens with lush tropical foliage, their stepped Greek Revival cornices set against a brilliant sky. Hedin's area diagrams, no doubt borrowed from Moellhausen and added to provide inducements for buyers, identify such neighborhood amenities as street railway tracks and stops, planked roads, nearby coffee houses, markets, wharves, churches, or schools. If after Moellhausen the genre expanded, after Hedin it was never the same. No one could outdo him.

Hedin worked both by himself and at various times with two partners with German-sounding names, V. Egloffstein and a Mr. Schlarbaum. Like Peter Paul Rubens, he seems to have had a studio where drawings were produced very obviously in his style, but neither signed nor dated. Whether these were by craven imitators or simply out of his *atelier* after his 1858 death, we cannot prove. One hundred and seventy-six plans fall into this category.

After the Civil War, the custom of making the distinctive Plan Book drawings continued without interruption in New Orleans until 1888. That year, one of the greatest plans in the collection, a 99 by 24 inch plantation tract complete with the image of a

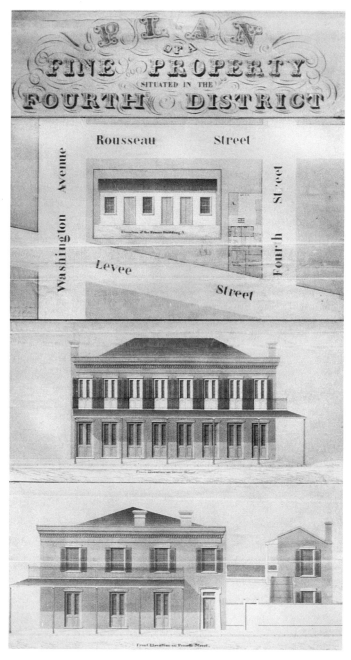

Fig. 4. Elevations of a red brick dry goods store and coffeehouse with dependency, showing attractive lettering and the fully developed style of C. A. Hedin during the 1850s. 'Plan of A / FINE PROPERTY / situated in the / FOURTH DISTRICT' [signed] 'New Orleans March 27th 1853 / C. A. Hedin / Civil Engineer.' Plan Book 49, Folio 11, New Orleans Notarial Archives. Courtesy, Custodian of Notarial Records, New Orleans, La.

raised, circa-1820 manor house surviving amid the subdivision of its own estate, was completed by Arthur George de Armas. After that, two years must elapse before one can count another water-color in the Plan Book collection, and following this, a decade. In 1901 another drawing appeared—indeed, there are thirteen completed between 1901 and 1918—but the technique had declined, along with the architecture it depicted. Blueprints, Van Dykes, sepias, and various other experiments with diazo now took center stage. Today the bluelines are still filed relentlessly, and we duly process them—but they are more likely to show a zoning proviso for a Wendy's parking lot than they are to show a building. Perhaps it is just as well. The archival drawings were born, grew, and died in one kind of place and time, and both are now gone.

CONCLUSION

While an armchair review of the highlights of this collection focuses attention on the drawings as art, it must be remembered that they are both more and less than that. Most fundamentally, they are legal documents. They reinforce the information in the notarial acts for whose ends they were generated, and the acts do the same. Sometimes they provide the only graphic representation of a lot in an entire chain of title, and every now and again must wake from their legal slumber to reassume for a moment their evidentiary value before retiring to the serene realm of history, art, and architecture.

Evidentiary value aside, the plans offer great potential for historic research. They depict a wide variety of building types, including Spanish colonial and Creole townhouses, Creole cottages and storehouses, Greek Revival and Italianate suburban houses, American-style row houses, granite-front American stores, warehouses, shotgun cottages, markets, street railway depots, kitchens, slave quarters, stables, poultry houses, cisterns, wells, and sheds. Plans with landscaping details may depict recognizable trees and flowering shrubs, walkways, gazebos, fences, little French *parterres*, vegetable gardens, or fruit arbors. Neighborhood amenities will include navigation canals, bridges, and frequently the cars and tracks of street railways. Plans from nearby states stress prominent topographical features such as water frontage, smaller rivers, and bayous. From the neighboring parishes or across the Mississippi River, we may find an occasional, if rare, plantation house. In all, it is an unparalleled resource for the study of architectural history, historic landscape design, graphic arts and color, technological history, social history, city planning, and topography

Like the city that gave birth to them, the plans came out of European traditions reshaped into something distinct unto New Orleans. The genre evolved in the context of the social and legal culture resting on a traditional Gallic base that was transformed in the currents of America. Perhaps 10,000 of these plans once existed, although the Archives has only half that. In any case, it is clear that without the notarial system of New Orleans, few if any would probably have survived, if they existed at all.

Set to Music:
The Engravers, Artists, and Lithographers
of New Orleans Sheet Music

FLORENCE M. JUMONVILLE

ROM THE TIME the city of New Orleans was founded in 1718, the procession of its history has marched to the beat of music. It was taught in a school founded by missionaries in 1725, and in the archives of the Ursuline nuns is a manuscript volume containing religious music composed in 1736 in the Crescent City to commemorate the Lenten season. The first documented performance of an opera occurred in 1796, and during the nineteenth century New Orleanians sustained a self-supporting resident opera company that provided some of the best opera available in America. At the French Opera House and other theaters and concert halls, throngs sought admittance. Historian John Smith Kendall claimed that 'on opera nights crowds competed for the upper, cheaper galleries at the Opera House so vigorously that coats were torn, hats crushed, and tempers ruffled; and then, ensconced in the coveted locations, sat for hours entranced, listening to the music with tears of delight streaming unashamedly down their faces.'[1]

1. Alfred E. Lemmon, '*Te Deum Laudamus*: Music in St. Louis Cathedral from 1725 to 1844,' in Glenn R. Conrad, ed., *Cross, Crozier, and Crucible: A Volume Celebrating the Bicentennial of a Catholic Diocese in Louisiana* ([New Orleans]: Archdiocese of New Orleans in Cooperation with the Center for Louisiana Studies, 1993), 490; Henry A. Kmen, 'Singing and Dancing in New Orleans: A Social History of the Birth and Growth of Balls and Opera, 1791–1841' (Ph.D. diss., Tulane University, 1961), iv, 92, 98–99; John Smith

FLORENCE JUMONVILLE is head librarian of the Historic New Orleans Collection.

After the United States bought the Louisiana Territory from France in 1803, enterprising Americans, lured by the prospect of opportunity, poured into the newly acquired region. The population, further swelled by emigrants from Santo Domingo and other countries, soared from approximately 7,000 in 1803 to 12,000 by 1806, and had doubled within four years.[2] The newcomers flooding onto the docks and streets of New Orleans included composers and musicians who would contribute to the city's musical heritage and persons who would aid their efforts by facilitating the physical production of sheet music that the composers wrote and the musicians played. Among the latter were Henri and Clementine Wehrmann, little more than newlyweds, who arrived from Paris in the fall of 1849 after a voyage of forty-eight days.[3] Because of this couple, the history of sheet music in New Orleans should be dated 'B.W.' and 'A.W.'—'Before Wehrmann' and 'After Wehrmann,' for she was an engraver and he a printer and lithographer who, during the next fifty years, individually or together would produce an estimated 8,000 pieces of sheet music.[4] Their contribution was substantial because their firm was the first to concentrate on the publication of music.

Kendall, 'New Orleans' Musicians of Long Ago,' *The Louisiana Historical Quarterly* 31 (January 1948), 130–31 (quotation).

2. These statistics appear in Robert Clemens Reinders, 'A Social History of New Orleans, 1850–1860' (Ph.D. diss., University of Texas at Austin, 1957), 6–7. Other estimates of the population in 1803 and 1806 vary.

3. 'Golden Wedding,' New Orleans *Times-Democrat* (October 23, 1898). The precise date of the Wehrmanns' arrival is not known, but family records in the possession of their granddaughter, Lise Wehrmann Wells of New Orleans, state that their first child, Henriette, was born in Paris on August 22, 1849. Considering the length of the voyage and assuming that Henriette was at least two weeks old when the family left France, they could not have arrived before late October.

4. John Smith Kendall quotes this estimate without citing his source ('Musicians of Long Ago,' 148). It has been repeated, apparently uncritically, by Peggy C. Boudreaux, 'Music Publishing in New Orleans in the Nineteenth Century' (M.A. thesis, Louisiana State University and Agricultural and Mechanical College, 1977), 1, and in *Encyclopaedia of New Orleans Artists, 1718–1918*, ed. John A. Mahé and Rosanne McCaffrey (New Orleans: Historic New Orleans Collection, 1987), 405. I have examined over 1,200 pieces to which the Wehrmanns contributed the music, the cover, or both. Based on the plate numbers which appear on many of those pieces, it can be determined that the Wehrmanns engraved between 4,500 and 5,000 pieces that bear plate numbers. A substantial quantity lack plate numbers, and it is indeed likely that another 3,000 pieces or more could have been pro-

As secular music became increasingly popular in the 1700s, a growing demand developed for sheet music, which provided the directions aspiring musicians needed. Sheet music publishing emerged in America during the latter half of the eighteenth century and by the late 1780s had been securely established in Boston, New York, Philadelphia, Baltimore, and Charleston. As the frontier moved westward, sheet music publishers and dealers followed it to Pittsburgh, Cincinnati, Cleveland, Chicago, St. Louis, and other towns both small and large including New Orleans.[5] Before the local production of sheet music began, the names of Crescent City music sellers appeared as secondary imprints on pieces of sheet music engraved and published elsewhere. This practice kept New Orleanians in contact with musical trends in other major cities and continued well into the nineteenth century.[6]

Conversely, publishers in other cities participated as secondary publishers of music that began to issue from the Crescent City in the 1850s. The earliest dated piece discovered thus far that bears a New Orleans imprint is 'Bounding Billows,' copyrighted on May 24, 1827, by Philadelphia publisher George Willig and sold in New Orleans by Emile Johns, who had begun selling sheet music the previous year.[7]

---

duced by the Wehrmanns. The pieces I have seen come from the substantial holdings of the Historic New Orleans Collection, the Louisiana Collection at Howard-Tilton Memorial Library at Tulane University (New Orleans), and Hill Memorial Library at Louisiana State University (Baton Rouge), as well as two small collections owned privately.

5. Richard F. French, 'The Dilemma of the Music Publishing Industry,' in Paul Henry Lang, ed., *One Hundred Years of Music in America* (New York: Grosset & Dunlap, 1961), 173; Richard J. Wolfe, *Early American Music Engraving and Printing: A History of Music Publishing in America from 1787 to 1825 with Commentary on Earlier and Later Practices* (Urbana: University of Illinois Press, 1980), 38; *The New Grove Dictionary of American Music*, s.v. 'Publishing and printing of music.'

6. Boudreaux, 'Music Publishing,' 102. See, for example, 'Donna Ada's Polka' by T. M. Brown, which was published in New York in 1873 by Wm. A. Pond & Co., in Chicago by Root & Lewis, in San Francisco by M. Gray, in Pittsburgh by H. Kleber & Bro., in Milwaukee by H. N. Hempsted, and in New Orleans by Louis Grunewald. More research into this cooperative publishing and distribution is needed.

7. John H. Baron, 'Paul Emile Johns of New Orleans: Tycoon, Musician, and Friend of Chopin,' in International Musicological Society, *Report of the Eleventh Congress* (Copenhagen: International Musicological Society, 1972), 246–50.

Lithography, introduced in the United States soon after 1800 and used extensively after 1825, freed printers from the restrictions of traditional engraving and typography. The process had reached New Orleans by 1822, but fifteen years passed before it became firmly ensconced. In 1837 the bilingual newspaper *L'Abeille (The Bee)*, heralding lithography as 'one of the brilliant discoveries of the age,' established a lithographic department from which a variety of lithographs and sheet music began to emerge.[8] 'Le doute,' a romance that apparently was issued in association with the January 21, 1838, issue of a weekly periodical entitled *La Créole*, is the earliest dated New Orleans–produced sheet music. Its cover was executed by local printers Jerome Bayon and Justin Sollée, but the music itself was lithographed by *The Bee*, which provided both music and cover for future issues.[9]

Others hastened to practice this new art. Emile Johns, who began to sell sheet music published in France and the northeastern United States in 1826, opened a printing office in New Orleans in 1834. With the advent of lithography, he established one of the first firms in the Crescent City. Born in Cracow and trained in Vienna as a concert pianist, he migrated to New Orleans in 1818 at the age of twenty to pursue a musical career. It took a different form than he had expected. E. Johns & Company, music sellers and stationers, was established in 1830, and he opened a printing office in 1834 to which he soon added lithography. Since Johns was active as a composer, it is not surprising that he would produce sheet music. 'Hark Maties Hark' is the only extant piece bearing his own imprint as a lithographer. The rest of the music that he composed or published was printed by other lithographers.[10]

8. 'Lithography at the Bee Office,' New Orleans *Bee*, April 5, 1837; Priscilla O'Reilly, 'A New Plane: Pre-Civil War Lithography' (Paper presented at the Nineteenth Annual North American Print Conference, New Orleans, April 29, 1987), 1–3.

9. Madame Saint-Clair, 'Le doute' (Nouvelle-Orléans: [s.n.], 21 Janvier 1838); also, e.g., Julien Pecarrere, '*Si l'avait su*' (Nouvelle-Orléans: [s.n.], 18 Février 1838).

10. Mrs. G. L. Poindexter, 'Hark Maties Hark' ([S.l.: s.n., c. 1839]); e.g., E. Johns, '*Oh! plaignez le pauvre orphelin,' publiée pour le bénefice des orphelins* (Nouvelle Orléans: Imprimé gratis chez Juls. Manouvrier & P. Snell, 18 Décembre 1839).

When Johns issued 'Jackson's Grand March' in 1840 in association with the commemoration of the twenty-fifth anniversary of
the Battle of New Orleans, he turned to Jean Houguenague for
lithography. Census records indicate that Houguenague was born
during the first decade of the nineteenth century, and city directories from 1841 through 1846 list him as a lithographic printer.[11]
Four pieces of sheet music by him have survived, each of which is
significant. 'Grand Tippecanoe March,' copyrighted in 1840, is
probably the earliest dated New Orleans sheet music that bears an
illustrated cover. 'National Waltzes,' copyrighted in 1839, was
distributed jointly by Emile Johns and Benjamin Casey, another
local vendor of sheet music whose business was established immediately after Johns's.[12] Casey engaged Houguenague to lithograph 'Old Rosin the Bow,' but he also published a number of
other pieces such as 'La Cachucha,' also undated but likely earlier,
that do not bear the imprint of a lithographer or engraver.

Jules Manouvrier arrived in New Orleans from Prussia at the
age of twenty two in 1838 and remained there until he died in
1875.[13] In addition to views of prominent buildings such as St.
Louis Cathedral and St. Mary's Church in Galveston, he lithographed maps and numerous pieces of sheet music. Manouvrier is
noteworthy as one of the few lithographers who worked both
'B.W.' and 'A.W.' He produced pieces such as the 'Buena Vista
March' and 'Une couronne de fleurs' between 1846 and 1852,
when he worked with Perez Snell to create both the music and the
covers. Snell, born during the last decade of the eighteenth century, was active in New Orleans as a printer and lithographer
from 1835 to 1852. Later Manouvrier produced the covers of
such pieces as 'La couronne imperiale' for which the Wehrmanns
engraved the music.[14]

11. *New Orleans Artists*, 190.
12. On Casey, see Boudreaux, 'Music Publishing,' 17–20.
13. *New Orleans Artists*, 252.
14. 'Buena Vista March' (New Orleans: Wm. T. Mayo, [c. 1848]); H. E. Lehmann, 'Une
couronne de fleurs' (Nouvelle Orléans: Wm. T. Mayo, [between 1846 and 1852]); L.
Gabici, 'Grand Triumphal March' ([New Orleans]: Wm. T. Mayo; [New Orleans]: J. E.
Benoit, [1847 or 1848]); H. E. Lehmann, 'La couronne imperiale de L'Étoile du Nord'

Louis Xavier Magny, like Manouvrier, worked in New Orleans before the Wehrmanns came and continued after they arrived. Magny, the first person in New Orleans to recognize their talent, was a native of Avignon who was born during the first decade of the nineteenth century. He arrived in New Orleans in the mid-1840s and remained active until his death in 1855,[15] lithographing prints of prominent buildings such as St. Louis Cathedral, numerous portraits, and book illustrations for *Rodolphe de Branchelièvre* by Charles Lemaître and others. Magny also produced some of the finest and most diverse sheet music covers of his time and place, such as 'The Rangers Lament for Poor Old Joe,' a Whig song that supporters of Millard Fillmore introduced in 1849. Some, like 'Polka aërienne,' bore relatively simple illustrations, while others were considerably more intricate. 'Valse du Tivoli,' for example, provides probably the only surviving illustration of a popular beer garden located just beyond the French Quarter. Textual accounts verify that the image is an accurate one. 'The Crescent Mazurka' was 'dedicated to the ladies of the Crescent City by the publisher,' E. A. Tyler, whose music store is depicted on the cover. Considering that Magny was noted for his portraits, it is not surprising that they appeared on some of his sheet music. An image of a little girl, possibly Nannie Nye Mayo, a daughter of music publisher William T. Mayo, graces the cover of 'The Golden Bird of Hope.' An unidentified 'Chatelaine' appears on the cover of a piece of that name, and a portrait of Madame Arraline Brooks, a local music teacher, graces the cover of 'Polka Quadrilles.' Both of those images were based on illustrations by Giovanni Tolti, who also did the art work for such lithographs as the 'Explosion of the Louisiana' between his arrival in New Orleans about 1849 and his death in 1860.[16]

(Nouvelle Orléans: A vendre chez les principaux Marchands de Musique, c. 1855); *New Orleans Artists*, 252, 359.

15. *Ibid.*, 250.

16. Charles Lemaître, *Rodolphe de Branchelièvre* (Nouvelle-Orléans: Imprimerie de J. L. Sollée, 1851); 'The Rangers Lament for Poor Old Joe' (New Orleans: Wm. T. Mayo, [1849]); Hubert Rolling, 'Polka aërienne' ([Nouvelle-Orléans]: En vente chez les Mar-

In 1846 Emile Johns sold his music business to William T. Mayo, who published many of the pieces Magny lithographed. The story is told that one day, probably in late 1849, Magny presented himself before Mayo, accompanied by 'a fair, blue-eyed slip of a girl scarcely more than five feet in height, with the daintiest of tiny hands, and said: "Monsieur, this lady is an engraver of music, and you will do well to give her work." Mr. Mayo looked at her incredulously. What! That fragile little girl an engraver! Those childish hands manage engravers' tools! He would not believe it. But since she insisted, he gave her something to engrave as a test.'[17] The young lady was the former Charlotte Marie Clementine Böhne, wife of Henri Wehrmann. Born in Paris in 1830, Clementine was then nineteen years old, and her husband, a native of Minden, Germany, was twenty-two. With their infant daughter, as well as her mother and brother, they had been drawn to New Orleans by family ties; Clementine's father, Auguste Böhne, had already established himself there as a music dealer. Perhaps he suggested to his daughter and son-in-law that the Crescent City would be a likely place in which to practice their talents.[18]

Although every accomplished young lady was expected to *play* the piano, engraving the music that enabled others to play was not a common talent for a woman. Astonishing though it may have seemed to Mayo, young Madame Wehrmann was a skilled engraver, and she passed his test effortlessly. When Clementine was a thirteen-year-old in Paris, 'according to the necessity of most young French girls, [she] was obliged to select a profession. She

chands de Musique, [between 1846 and 1852]); Hubert Rolling, 'Valse de Tivoli' ([New Orleans: s.n., [between 1846 and 1852]); 'The Crescent Mazurka' ([New Orleans]: E. A. Tyler, [n.d.]); Thomas J. Martin, 'The Golden Bird of Hope' ([S.l.: s.n.], c1850); H. E. Lehmann, 'La chatelaine' (Nouvelle Orléans: Chez H. E. Lehmann, et chez tous les principaux Marchands de Musique, [between 1846 and 1852]); Michael Hoffner, 'Polka quadrilles' (New Orleans: Wm. T. Mayo, [between 1846 and 1852]); *New Orleans Artists*, 377.

17. 'Musical History of Louisiana.' New Orleans *Times-Democrat* (October 31, 1909), sec. 3, p. 1.

18. *New Orleans Artists*, 405, 406.

had no taste for millinery, saw no future as a manipulator of wax flowers, and began to consider the art of engraving music, a study that soon took possession of the young girl, who gave three years services to her instructors for her apprenticeship.'[19] It is probable that her father was associated with the music business in Paris and that she did not select music engraving arbitrarily.

Following Magny's advice, Mayo gave the Wehrmanns work, and so did virtually all of the city's music publishers, including the 'big four': A. E. Blackmar; Louis Grunewald; Philip Werlein, who bought Mayo's business in 1852; and Junius Hart, who came a bit later than these others. Their fame spread beyond New Orleans, and so did their work; Wehrmann imprints appeared on sheet music published in Vicksburg, Natchez, Mobile, and other cities.[20] The 'A.W.' period of New Orleans music history was flourishing.

Three different Wehrmann imprints, discounting insignificant variations, appear on sheet music they produced: those of Madame Wehrmann, those of Henri Wehrmann, and those which read 'Wehrmann' or 'Wehrmann Engraver.' One of the earliest Wehrmann imprints I have found to date, that of Madame, appears on the last page of a piece of music published by Mayo in 1850. Entitled 'Sea Serpent Polka,' this piece bears a cover lithographed by Magny that is one of the most extraordinary produced in mid-nineteenth-century New Orleans and, in its day, was considered 'rather a shocking thing.'[21] It depicts a serpent with a man's head and forked tongue floating on the surface of the Mississippi River at New Orleans. The face was rumored

19. Unidentified newspaper clipping in Wehrmann scrapbook in possession of Lise Wehrmann Wells of New Orleans.

20. E.g., Basile Barès, 'Temple of Music' (New Orleans: Blackmar & Co., c1871); E. Bischoff, 'Crispino e la comare valse' (New Orleans: Louis Grünewald, c1866); Auguste Davis, '135 Canal Street Waltz' (New Orleans: Philip Werlein, c1877); Harry Graves, 'Sweet Eyes of Blue' (New Orleans: Junius Hart, c1891); E. E. Osgood, 'One of My Waltzes' (Vicksburg, Miss.: Blackmar & Brother, c1860); Robert Meyer, 'Irma' (Natchez: A. Dies, c1859); William Herz, 'Secession March' (Mobile, Ala.: J. H. Snow; Louisville: D. P. Faulds & Co.; New Orleans: A. E. Blackmar & Bro., c1861).

21. Eliza Ripley, *Social Life in Old New Orleans; Being Recollections of My Girlhood* (New York: D. Appleton and Co., 1912), 148.

to be a likeness of the composer, Maurice Strakosch, who resided in New Orleans and supplemented his income from teaching music by writing it.[22]

A newspaper clipping that describes the elderly Madame Wehrmann as 'small, white-haired, with large, expressive blue eyes, and the soul of music in her features' also outlines her technique. 'The engraving is done on plaques of metal composed of tin and lead, of silvery appearance. The ledger lines are scraped along with an instrument with the aid of a ruler of iron; the notes and accidentals and other musical characters like die in the tops of iron [are] placed over the designed spot and struck, leaving the effect upon the clear surface. The supplementary and note-lines, the ties, quavers, rests and clefs are graven in this way; then the plates are delivered to the printer, who may produce a million copies from it. There is some art in the work of these plaques, and much skill and familiarity with the groundwork of music; and it has all become second-nature of Mme. Wehrmann, who loves her profession, and can readily produce three engraved plates during a day.'[23]

Those pieces which bear the Wehrmann imprint without a given name almost certainly were engraved by Madame Wehrmann. Less is known about Henri's background than about his wife's. He is usually described as a printer,[24] and it is likely that he just operated the presses, but his imprint appears on roughly as many pieces as his wife's. Obviously all of the music was produced using the same equipment and the same methods. The possibilities are that Clementine, as a sort of ghost-engraver, produced the music which bears Henri's name as head of the firm or, considering that his imprint appears exclusively on music from 1880 and later, that through the years he learned the art of engraving music from his wife. Meager evidence, chiefly the contemporary references to Henri as a printer and not as an engraver, suggests the former theory.

22. Kendall, 'Musicians of Long Ago,' 134.
23. Unidentified newspaper clipping in Wehrmann scrapbook in possession of Lise Wehrmann Wells of New Orleans.
24. 'Golden Wedding.'

A significant number of pieces of sheet music share the characteristics of having been printed by the Wehrmanns but lack imprints. Covering virtually the entire period in which the Wehrmanns were active and including a variety of compositions, these pieces undoubtedly issued from their shop. It is possible but highly improbable that employees or apprentices executed some of the work. More likely Clementine produced those pieces as well as those which bear imprints, although no information survives that would explain why some pieces are unsigned. Except for other family members who will be discussed below, no other engravers of the period could be found whose backgrounds included working with them. Given their prominence and apparent popularity in late nineteenth-century New Orleans, it is likely that former employees would have boasted of the association and, as the years passed, been sought out to give newspaper interviews entitled something like 'My Years with the Wehrmanns.'

Before the Civil War various lithographers produced covers which were as different as the music plates were similar. Magny, for example, lithographed the cover of the 'Eclipse Polka,' which depicts the composer, Henssler. Elaborate lettering characterized covers by Charles J. Stevens, a New Yorker who, during the 1850s when he was active in New Orleans,[25] also illustrated books such as *Bliss of Marriage; or, How to Get a Rich Wife*[26] and *A History of the Proceedings in the City of New Orleans, on the Occasion of the Funeral Ceremonies in Honor of Calhoun, Clay and Webster, Which Took Place on Thursday, December 9th, 1852.*[27] 'Oratorial Grand March' reproduces Dionis Simon's rendering of the monument on Canal Street that honored the popular politician Henry Clay. Simon, a native of Germany, was active in New Orleans from 1857 until his

25. F. Henssler, 'Eclipse-polka' (New Orleans: Wm. T. Mayo, c1852); Theodore von La Hache, 'Grand Dedication Cantata' (New Orleans: H. D. Hewitt; Boston: O. Ditson; New-York: Wm. Hall & Son, c1853); *New Orleans Artists*, 365.
26. S. S. Hall, *Bliss of Marriage; or, How to Get a Rich Wife* (New Orleans: J. B. Steel, 1858).
27. (New Orleans: General Committee of Arrangements, 1853).

death in 1876 at the age of 46.[28] He collaborated with Tolti to create the cover of a piece of music composed by a slave named Basile.[29] Another German, Benedict Simon, combined talents on some covers with Louis Lucien Pessou, an African-American born in New Orleans in 1825 and active as a lithographer from 1853 to 1868. Benedict Simon was one of the city's earliest and finest color lithographers and is best remembered for a series of thirty-two views of local buildings, including an especially vivid depiction of his own establishment.[30]

In the early 1860s Jules Lion, a free man of color, contributed the art work for some of the most noteworthy music covers that emanated from New Orleans. Lion was born in France about 1811 and came to New Orleans in late 1836 or early 1837, remaining active as a painter, sketch artist, and lithographer until his death in 1866. Probably his first employment there was as one of the two sketch artists employed by *L'Abeille* to execute drawings from which lithographs were made. Noted for his portraiture, Lion produced a series of lithographs including among his subjects both prominent and average citizens. Also a photographer, Lion is credited with introducing the daguerreotype process to the Crescent City in 1840. None of his daguerreotypes is known to survive.[31]

Not surprisingly, most of Lion's music covers also portrayed persons and buildings. Ironically, many of them, such as the 'General Joseph E. Johnston Quick March,' illustrated Confederate figures. 'Parade March and Quick Step' is dedicated to the fifth company of the Washington Artillery, and three members of the company appear on the cover. The couple standing before a

28. Thomas J. Martin, 'Oratorial Grand March' (New Orleans: F. Hartel, 1860); *New Orleans Artists*, 353.

29. Basile [Barès], 'Grande polka des chasseurs a pied, de la Louisiane' (Nouvelle Orléans: En vente chez les Marchands de Musique, c1860).

30. F. R. Prohl, 'The American Flag' (New Orleans: P. P. Werlein & Co.; New York: Wm. Hall & Son; Philadelphia: G. André & Co.; Boston: O. Ditson & Co., c1858); *New Orleans Artists*, 353.

31. Charles East, 'Jules Lion's New Orleans,' *The Georgia Review* 40 (Winter 1986), passim; *New Orleans Artists*, 238–39.

Confederate flag on one series cover can be identified as Harry Macarthy, who composed 'Missouri!' and the other pieces listed, and his wife Lottie Estelle. 'Free Market Waltz' bears the only extant image of the structure built as a waterworks after it was remodelled for use as a distribution center where Confederate women whose menfolks were off fighting received free foodstuffs contributed by upriver plantation owners.[32]

For several years, beginning with the occupation of New Orleans by federal troops on May 1, 1862, the local music business was in turmoil. Union soldiers confiscated Philip Werlein's stock and sold it at public auction, and the firm ceased all operations until the autumn of 1865. The story is told that the Wehrmanns were at Werlein's when the soldiers arrived, and Henri, 'knowing their penchant for acquiring booty, contrived to camouflage the fine pianos under a huge tarpaulin, surrounding them with whatever warehouse material he could find. Expecting to find the expensive pianos displayed on the floors of the store, the soldiers did not bother to look at the heap of "junk" that hid . . . [them].' It was with those instruments that Werlein was able eventually to reestablish his operations. Grunewald also was forced out of business. Similarly, A. E. Blackmar's stock was raided and his Confederate copyrights confiscated by order of General Benjamin Butler. This situation impelled Blackmar and his brother Henry to relocate their headquarters, which Henry managed in Augusta, Georgia, while A. E. remained in New Orleans. Despite these obstacles, the Blackmar firm almost certainly was the most prolific publisher of Confederate sheet music.[33]

32. Adolphus Brown, 'Genl. Joseph E. Johnston Manassas Quick March' (New-Orleans: A. E. Blackmar & Bro., c1861); Theodore von La Hache, 'Parade March and Quick Step' (New Orleans: P. P. Werlein & Halsey, c1861); Harry Macarthy, 'Missouri' (New Orleans: A. E. Blackmar & Bro., c1861), 'Free Market Waltz' (New Orleans: Louis Grunewald, c1862).

33. Richard B. Harwell, *Confederate Music* (Chapel Hill: University of North Carolina Press, 1950), 10–11, 17–24; 'Have You Ever Tried to Hide a Piano?,' unidentified newspaper clipping ([1942]) in Wehrmann scrapbooks (quotation). Harwell describes the Blackmar concern as numerically the leader in Confederate music publishing, with nearly twice the output of its nearest competitor (232 pieces; Schreiner & Son of Macon and Savannah issued 121). Because, however, many additional pieces have come to light in the

The Wehrmanns' output dwindled during most of the war years and immediately after the South's surrender. Of the dated pieces they engraved that I have seen, at least thirty were published in each of the years 1860, 1861, and 1869. By this last date Louisiana had been formally readmitted to the Union, although occupation troops remained in New Orleans until 1877. Except in 1863, when a high of twenty-four pieces were issued, annual production from 1862 through 1868 stood at two-thirds or less of its antebellum level. After 1864 this can be attributed in part to the major publishers' new tendency to commission out-of-state engravers to produce some of their music. The cover of the 'Crescent Hall Polka,' for example, was lithographed by local J. H. Boehler, but the music was engraved by Oakes—which Oakes has not yet been determined. Blackmar had a particularly close association with Clayton of New York, and other distant engravers contributed other pieces.[34]

Some pieces, of course, continued to be engraved by the Wehrmanns, often with covers by William H. Leeson, a prolific lithographer of sheet music covers who was primarily known as a photographer. With the advent of color lithography, Thomas Fitzwilliam made such work a specialty, and publisher Junius Hart often employed him to produce bright and colorful covers. Worthy of special mention is the 'Mexican Music' series, which Hart published after the Mexican Military Band's astonishing popularity during and after the World's Industrial and Cotton Centennial Exposition in 1885. These pieces would influence the early jazz musicians; according to Jelly Roll Morton, 'If you can't manage to put tinges of Spanish in your tunes, you will never be able to get the right seasoning, I call it, for jazz.'[35]

more than forty years since Harwell's work was published, we cannot accept this assessment without qualification or further investigation.

34. Theodore von La Hache, 'Crescent Hall Polka' (New Orleans: L. Grünewald, c1866). Other examples include J. W. Groschel, 'Sing Me a Switzer Song of Love,' and Morgan C. Kennedy, 'Birdie Schottisch' (New Orleans: Blackmar & Co., 1865); L. Hampel, 'Mount Hermon Schottisch,' and F. W. Smith, 'The Girl with the Calico Dress' (New Orleans: Blackmar & Co., 1866); Robert Meyer, 'How Can I Leave Thee' (New Orleans: Louis Grunewald, 1866).

35. Thomas L. Morgan and William Barlow, *From Cakewalks to Concert Halls: An*

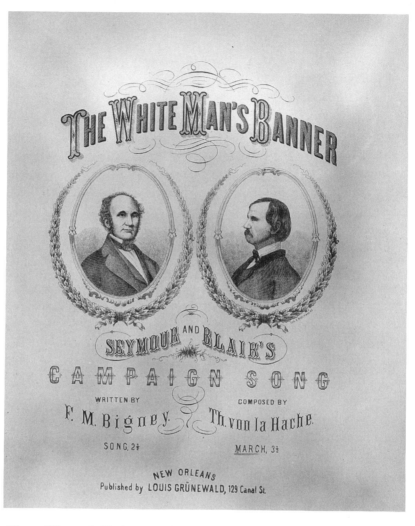

Fig. 1. Th. von la Hache, *The White Man's Banner, Seymour and Blair's Campaign Song* [Litho. H. Wehrmann N.O.], New Orleans: Louis Grunewald. American Antiquarian Society.

Fig. 2. Theod. von la Hache, *Silverspoons Schottisch* [Litho. H. Wehrmann N.O.],
New Orleans: Louis Grunewald. American Antiquarian Society.

Almost from the time they arrived in New Orleans, the Wehrmanns had been publishing sheet music themselves, in addition to producing it for Blackmar, Grunewald, and others. Often they enhanced their publications with covers by Louis F. Gery. Gery, a native of France, was born about 1830 and was active in New Orleans from 1850 until 1890 as an engraver and printer, but all of his dated sheet music, such as 'The Bell Crevasse' dedicated to Clementine Wehrmann, predates the Civil War.[36]

No lithographer claimed credit for the cover of 'Pic Nic Polka,' copyrighted in 1854 by its composer, the prolific and popular Theodore von La Hache. Although it was printed in blue, the imprint—that of Louis Grunewald—was added in black, after the original printing. Apparently the Wehrmanns kept plates in stock for some pieces that, in most instances, were in the public domain or for which Henri owned the copyright. They stood ready to add the imprint of any publisher or dealer who ordered in quantity. Multiple copies exist of a substantial number of such pieces, one copy without an imprint and each of the others with the imprint of a different publisher. For example, three copies of 'Minuit' by Basile Barès, the former slave composer, exist, one bearing Grunewald's imprint, another with Blackmar's, and a third without an imprint.[37]

The Wehrmanns' publishing endeavors burgeoned after the Civil War, and Henri became a major publisher of sheet music. Now he was responsible for commissioning covers, as well as for seeing to the engraving and printing of the music. At about the same time—around 1869—Henri's younger brother Hermann arrived in New Orleans, probably with his wife Henrietta, and briefly shared Henri's address. Like Henri, Hermann was a

---

Illustrated History of African American Popular Music from 1895 to 1930 (Washington: Elliott & Clark Publishing, 1992), 33.

36. N. A. Barbé, 'The Bell Crevasse' (New Orleans: P. P. Werlein & Co., c1858); *New Orleans Artists*, 155.

37. Basile Barès, 'Minuit' (New Orleans: A. E. Blackmar, c1873); Basile Barès, 'Minuit' (New Orleans: Louis Grunewald, c1873); Basile Barès, 'Minuit' ([S.l.: s.n.], c1873).

printer and lithographer, and between them the brothers created the covers for numerous pieces of sheet music during the last third of the nineteenth century. Hermann apparently remained with his brother only until he was able to establish his own firm. For a brief period in the late 1880s, Henri and Clementine's son Clement worked with his father.[38] In addition to music, Henri lithographed maps, a lengthy volume of plans of each square block of the third district of New Orleans, and Mardi Gras memorabilia, including a 1875 proclamation of Rex, King of Carnival

Among other pieces of music published by Henri and engraved by Clementine was 'Stella Waltz,' one of a number of pieces composed by Henry, the youngest of their seven children, born in 1870. By the age of seventeen, he already had several published works to his credit, including some of the few pieces of sheet music composed for instruments other than the piano. His contribution to the family enterprise went beyond composing music, for beginning in the late 1880s he also executed art work for many covers. He enjoyed widespread acclaim as a musician, composer, and teacher until his death in 1956, and he is still remembered in New Orleans some forty years later.[39]

As the twentieth century dawned, the sun began to set on the New Orleans music publishing industry. Henri's 1905 obituary recalled: 'Twenty-five years ago his publication and handiwork were utilized in every city of the United States, but the rapid advancement in the art, and the utilization of movable types in printing cheap music, reduced the demand for metallic plate and stone work, and his business decreased in consequence.'[40] The Wehrmanns faced competition from other firms, such as the Standard Music and Photo-Litho Company, and lithographers like Odbert V. Greend who, like the Wehrmanns themselves, operated independently. Nevertheless, the Wehrmann imprint con-

38. *New Orleans Artists*, 406–7; Boudreaux, 'Music Publishing,' 36.
39. Henry Wehrmann Jr., 'Stella Waltz' ([S.l.: s.n.], c1889); *New Orleans Artists*, 406–7. Although this and other publications give Wehrmann's date of birth as 1871, family records in the possession of his daughter, Lise Wells, state that he was born in 1870.
40. 'Henri Wehrmann, Sr., Dead,' New Orleans *Times-Democrat*, September 14, 1905.

tinued to appear at least until 1899, although with decreasing frequency. As noted above, Henri died in 1905 and Clementine in 1911; each was ill just for a few days.[41]

'New Orleans was, in the nineteenth century, a cultural center without equal in the South,'[42] where concert halls and theaters were patronized by a large, music-loving public. At home, young ladies cultivated the skills of piano-playing and singing, and they accumulated dozens, in some instances perhaps even hundreds, of pieces of sheet music: dance music, prominently including polkas, galops, and the very popular waltzes; patriotic Confederate pieces; marches and quicksteps; religious music; vocal music; and substantial quantities of works from opera. Some of the city's finest lithographers and engravers contributed their talents to the creation of that sheet music, but none sustained the sort of establishment where a corps of apprentices practiced the art. Even the Wehrmanns, whose extensive output would suggest that they had help, maintained a family operation. Considering how far-reaching was their influence, we can but speculate what could have happened had there been no Civil War and had they sought to expand their business. As it is, we are left to study the music and the sparse data left behind in an effort to understand better the major contribution these two and their colleagues made to the cultural life of New Orleans, the South, and the nation.

41. *Ibid.*; 'Death Comes to Mrs. Wehrmann,' clipping from unidentified newspaper, March 31, 1911.
42. Boudreaux, 'Music Publishing,' iv.

Art, Industry, and Education in Prang's Chromolithograph Company

MICHAEL CLAPPER

C HROMOLITHOGRAPHS are largely forgotten nowadays, but in the late nineteenth century they were a prominent part of visual culture.[1] The shortened term 'chromo' was coined by Louis Prang in 1865 as a name for his full-color facsimiles of paintings. The bulk of the images that Prang and other chromolithographic firms produced were not fine art reproductions, but product labels, posters, business cards, and advertise-

My thanks to Michael Leja and Amelia Rauser for their comments and criticisms. Thanks also to Georgia B. Barnhill and Caroline Sloat for their assistance in editing the manuscript. I am grateful to the American Antiquarian Society for a Kate B. and Hall J. Peterson Fellowship which aided my research, to the Society's exceptionally helpful staff, and to the organizers and supporters of the Society's 1993 conference on 'The Cultivation of Artists in Nineteenth-Century America' at which I presented an earlier version of this essay.

1. The most substantial scholarly treatment of chromolithographs remains Peter C. Marzio, *The Democratic Art; Pictures for a 19th-Century America* (Boston: David R. Godine, 1979). His work has been a catalyst for my own, and I recommend it to readers interested in a general discussion of chromolithographs. Marzio deals with Prang extensively in chapters 6 and 7, 94–115. Also see Katharine Morrison McClinton, *The Chromolithographs of Louis Prang* (New York: Clarkson N. Potter, 1973).

2. In its early years L. Prang and Company (and Prang and Mayer before 1860) was primarily a commercial printing firm specializing in labels. See Mary Margaret Sittig, 'L. Prang & Company: Fine Art Publishing,' unpublished M.A. thesis, George Washington University, 1970, 29. The American Antiquarian Society in Worcester, Mass., has an extensive collection of examples. After 1875 Christmas cards were the staple of Prang's printing business ('Autobiography of Louis Prang,' in Sittig, 154).

MICHAEL CLAPPER is a Ph.D. candidate in the Department of Art History at Northwestern University. His dissertation, 'Popularizing Art in Boston, 1865–1910,' examines the Prang chromolithograph company and the Museum of Fine Arts, Boston, as early examples of institution's seeking to educate a broad audience to the material and spiritual benefits of art.

Fig. 1. A product label for Leckerli de Basle, manufactured by J. J. Blaser, Boston, is an example of Prang's early commercial work. American Antiquarian Society.

ments. Prang made his reputation on fine art reproductions and most of his money on less ambitious commercial work (fig. 1).[2] Chromolithography attracted the most media comment as a medium for reproducing fine art and, while many commentators were not convinced that chromolithographs were themselves art, the enthusiasm for these prints was plain. This enthusiasm was not limited to journalists; the public demand for chromos was tremendous.[3] Louis Prang, who came to the United States as a skilled craftsman, succeeded in combining business and art by using industrialized production methods and mass marketing.

Prang was born in Europe and learned his skills, interests, and

3. For a discussion of responses to and debates over chromos, see Michael Clapper, 'The Chromo and the Art Museum: Popular and Elite Art Institutions in Late Nineteenth-Century America,' in Christopher Reed, ed., *Domesticity and Modernism* (London: Thames and Hudson, 1996).

tastes there.[4] When he emigrated to the United States in 1850 (forced to flee his involvement in the revolution of 1848), he subscribed to its democratic beliefs in two important respects. First, Prang came to believe that art could and should be democratized. This belief was based not only on the positive valuation of art as a product and sign of culture, but on a particularly American definition of its cultural infrastructure in contrast to the aristocratic institutions of Europe.[5] Second, Prang shared the American faith in the 'self-made man,' the idea that virtuous, ambitious individuals could succeed economically and socially regardless of their beginnings.[6] For Prang, these two beliefs taken together meant that public service and self-interest were not at odds with one another.

Prang arrived in the United States as a skilled laborer, not an entrepreneur, and much less a philanthropist. To make a living, he tried a number of ventures, first as a partner in a firm publishing architectural drawings, then in another partnership producing fine leatherwork, then for several years as a wood engraver, before forming a partnership in a lithographic business with Julius Mayer in 1856. This firm became L. Prang and Co. in 1860, when Prang bought out Mayer's interest.[7] As one job or partnership af-

4. Sittig includes an unpublished manuscript autobiography by Prang as an appendix, 123–56, as well as providing her own version of Prang's biography based largely on Prang's manuscript. Though Sittig dates the manuscript to c. 1874 (Sittig, 123), internal evidence, as Marzio notes (246, note 7), dates the manuscript to the late 1880s or later, and structural similarities relate it to a biography of Prang printed in the *Lithographer's Journal* in January 1892. In the autobiography Prang refers to 'the X-mas card period' (which ran from the late 1870s through the 1880s) in the past tense and mentions the formation of the Prang Educational Company, which did not occur until 1882.

5. The tension between art and republicanism and the persistent fear that art was a luxury that could lead to moral corruption are discussed in Neil Harris, *The Artist in American Society; The Formative Years, 1790–1860* (New York: G. Braziller, 1966), 28–53.

6. On the self-made man, see John G. Cawelti, *Apostles of the Self-Made Man* (Chicago: University of Chicago Press, 1965) and Irvin G. Wyllie, *The Self-Made Man in America; the Myth of Rags to Riches* (New York: The Free Press, 1966). The concept of the 'self-made man' extolled the virtues of ambition, self-reliance, and determined action in the public realm of capitalist business. Given the strong masculine coding of these character traits in the nineteenth century, this ideal of personal advancement excluded women. In addition, expectations and regulations about women's social roles closed many opportunities for public advancement to them.

7. Sittig, 'L. Prang & Company,' 134–47.

ter another broke up, Prang got his education as a commercial artist and business person in a typical way—he learned by experience, within the unforgiving strictures of the market. His attempts to apply his craft skills honed his business skills.

The key to Prang's success was his ability to define and serve markets. For example, at the outset of the Civil War, Prang's and other printing firms struggled, often unsuccessfully, to survive. Out of work, Prang acted on a suggestion to print a detailed pictorial map of the Fort Sumter battle site just as the conflict unfolded. His first effort quickly sold 40,000 copies at twenty-five cents each. Recognizing success, Prang went on to produce other similar maps.[8] He continued to develop new markets through hunches and trial and error.[9]

Louis Prang's company began to make chromolithographic reproductions of fine art oil paintings in 1866, and until the perfection of photomechanical printing in the 1890s chromolithography was the main means of making reproducible color images for artistic or commercial purposes. Between 1866 and 1876 Prang and other publishers sold hundreds of thousands of 'chromos' throughout the United States. Within five years, he lamented that the success of his chromos had led other publishers to call every colored lithograph a chromo and reasserted his own more rigorous definition: 'What a Chromo really ought to be, that is, *an imitation of an oil painting so close as to require a careful examination to detect the difference.*'[10]

These high-quality reproductions opened up a vibrant new market that offered artists opportunities for employment and recognition. Machine production and capitalist marketing techniques when applied to the fine arts fundamentally changed the way art was made and used (fig. 2). Prang employed an existing pool of skilled labor, including immigrants who had learned their

8. *Ibid.*, 40–41.
9. In the late 1870s a combination of cheaper competitors and a saturated market forced Prang to curtail production of chromos. He adapted chromolithography to a new purpose and pioneered the modern greeting card industry.
10. Sittig, 'L. Prang & Company,' 25–26; *Prang's Chromo* 2 (8) (Sept. 1870), 5.

Fig. 2. L. Prang & Co.'s Art Publishing House, the new factory built in 1868.
American Antiquarian Society.

skills in Europe, and organized this labor force in a traditional
workshop. Hand-craft skills and a judicious eye were required,
despite the mechanized processes of industrial mass production.

The image of *The Lithographer* from Prang's series of prints of
Trades and Occupations (1875) illustrates the steps in the process
(fig. 3). Unlike painters, lithographers worked collaboratively.
Even the most prominent chromolithographers might draw only
some of the many stones or plates required to make the finished
print, and several other individuals would be involved in the
process of printing. The figure on the left prepares a lithographic
stone by sliding it over another such stone, using progressively
finer grit to 'grain' the stones. This procedure removed the thin
layer of chemically altered stone which still held the last image
printed, readying the valuable stones to accept a new image.[11]

11. By the time *The Lithographer* was published, this traditional method of working was
being superseded. In the early 1870s the Prang company pioneered the use of thin, pre-
grained zinc plates instead of the more expensive and unwieldy limestone slabs.

Fig. 3. *The Lithographer*, plate 5, in L. Prang, *Trades and Occupations* (Boston: L. Prang & Company, 1875). American Antiquarian Society.

Arthur Tait's *Pointer and Quail* (fig. 4) and *Spaniel and Woodcock* are visible on the stone at the grainer's feet, now ready to be reused. The lithographic artist seated at center near a window is intent on drawing on his stone. The original oil painting that served as a model is propped against the partition, and above the painting is tacked a ghostly proof image showing the cumulative effect of the layers of transparent color already printed. On the other side of the partition a printer is applying ink to a stone resting on the bed of a manual press, having used the chemicals from the table behind him to prepare the stone to receive the ink.

Lithography was learned in the shop through apprenticeship. Young novices were paid very little while they learned the basics of the craft and performed menial labor; they gradually assumed professional responsibilities after a period of service. Work experience and demonstrated skill were the keys to better pay and more demanding jobs. In-house artists created original designs primarily for the commercial work, labels, posters, and other advertising pieces, as well as greeting cards and 'art studies' for am-

Fig. 4. *Pointer and Quail* after Arthur Tait, 1869. American Antiquarian Society.

ateurs to use as models. Prang offered these artists steady employment and promotion as their technical facility and invention developed. It was this team of craftsmen whose skills became outdated with the development of mechanical or photographic means to perform most of their tasks.[12]

Prang published roughly 160 of his top-of-the-line images, *Prang's American Chromos*, between 1866 and 1876. He usually acquired completed works for reproduction, rather than commissioning paintings or having lithographers in his employ create original designs. The painters whose pictures Prang reproduced

12. Leeds Armstrong Wheeler, *Armstrong & Company, Artistic Lithographers* (Boston: Boston Public Library, 1982) gives rich, detailed insight into the organization, working habits, and sense of community of artists working in a lithographic company. See also Marzio, *The Democratic Art*, 149–153, for some specific figures on and images of work within lithographic shops.

were for the most part established artists and well known at the time, including Albert Bierstadt, Eastman Johnson, John George Brown, Arthur Tait, and Benjamin Champney. Most of them were members of the National Academy of Design or other leading artists' organizations.[13] Prang also offered a few works by acclaimed European painters, providing an added air of sophistication. While the chromolithograph industry offered new opportunities and opened occupational niches for American artists, it did not necessarily provide solutions to an artist's chronic problem of finding sufficient financial and cultural support for his efforts.

Prang's involvement in image making was limited but significant. The chromolithographs that his company produced were not by his hand, nor specifically of his conception, but he played a decisive role by selecting the images and shaping their cultural significance. Nor was Prang directly involved in the formation or training of fine artists. He did not function as an art director might today, suggesting changes in an image in process. The painters were rarely chromolithographers themselves; only a few had more than a basic idea of what would reproduce well. In rare instances, a chromolithographer might paint the image to be reproduced. William Harring, who was one of Prang's chief lithographers, painted *Kitchen Bouquet* (a still life with tomatoes) and some of Prang's smaller images, but this was exceptional. At most, an artist whose work had been successful as a chromolithograph might be asked to produce more works in a similar vein. Arthur Tait is a good example. After the success of his *Group of Chickens* in 1866, he painted and Prang issued *Group of Ducklings* (1866) and *Group of Quail* (1867). Related works were produced in later years.[14]

Prang would purchase one or more pictures from an artist and suggest that their reputation would be enhanced and patronage increased. He wrote, 'One good chromo after a popular picture

13. Sittig, 'L. Prang & Company,' 57. This study lists artists whose work Prang published between 1866 and 1876 on pages 60–67.
14. Sittig lists Prang's pre-1876 chromos after Tait, 66. Also see my note 18 below.

will do more to give fame to an artist than a dozen pictures hidden away in private galleries. And yet, where an unknown artist will sell *one* picture to a collector, an artist whose name has become famous will sell six. So the way to the private gallery lies through the chromo.'[15] Prang's claim that chromolithographs would foster an artist's career, even indirectly, was not validated by many artists' experience. In an unpublished autobiography Prang remarked that 'Up to this day there are a number of artists whose work I cannot obtain for reproduction, they fearing the influence upon their sales.' As it turned out, their fear that the availability of reproductions—which many buyers enjoyed nearly if not fully as much as paintings which cost roughly ten to one hundred times as much = could slow some artists' sales noticeably was justified. Arthur Tait told Prang that 'I find more and more that I must go into them [chromos], largely to repay me for the losses they have caused me in destroying the sales of my specialities [sic], *as they have done completely.*' Prang preferred to think that the sale of chromos based on an artist's work would aid sales of oil paintings, but Tait spoke from experience.[16]

Even artists whose works enjoyed great popularity as chromos could deplore their dealings with Prang. The artist Benjamin Stone, whose paintings led to some of Prang's early successes, claimed that, in its first year alone, *Harvest* had netted Prang $21,000 at $5.00 per chromo. Stone received none of this money, having sold the painting (and the right to reproduce it) to Prang outright for $50.00.[17] This arrangement, with no royalties for the artist, was common practice for Prang.

In a less typical case Prang offered Tait, one of his most popu-

15. *Prang's Chromo* 2 (8) (Sept. 1870), 4.

16. 'Autobiography of Louis Prang' in Sittig, 'L. Prang & Company,' 152; Warder H. Cadbury, *Arthur Fitzwilliam Tait: Artist in the Adirondacks* (Newark: University of Delaware Press, 1986), 84.

17. Catherine Campbell, 'Benjamin Bellows Grant Stone: A Forgotten American Artist,' *New York Historical Society Quarterly* (January 1978), 62: 22–42. Campbell quotes Stone's notes: '*Harvest* painted Nov. 1867—published 1869 . . . Sold at auction 1879 for $125 . . . Most popular chromo ever published. Sales the first year amounted to $21,000. Average sales from 1869 to 1878 $12,000 per year' (38). Even if Stone exaggerated, it is clear that Prang dealt with artists to his own advantage.

lar artists, a royalty of ten percent of gross sales of *Group of Chickens*, an offer Prang considered 'generous.' This royalty was to be paid only for the first two years the print was on sale, though Prang kept some prints in stock for decades. Tait advised Prang not to refer to such a proposition as generous if he wished their professional relationship to continue to be congenial.[18]

To appreciate the cultural significance of chromolithography in the popularization of art, it is necessary to set it in the context of an ongoing national interest in art and efforts to create art institutions and encourage American artists. As art institutions struggled to move beyond simply existing to making substantive contributions to an artistic community, funding was a nagging problem. Government aid, though hoped for, didn't materialize, so it wasn't possible to establish academies for training artists.[19] The tiny circle of persons who were wealthy and interested in art did not provide enough of an economic base to support sustained artistic production. The question those who wished to promote art would have to face was how to interest a broad audience and get them to participate.

Prang's enterprise brought art and business together on a grand scale. There were changes in the ways artists acquired their skills, and in the ways those skills were put to use by Prang and other art entrepreneurs. As a result, labor within this new 'art business' became more specialized on an individual level and more integrated on a corporate level. He and other chromolithograph publishers made art much more widely available while redefining 'art.'

18. Cadbury, *Arthur Fitzwilliam Tait*, 78. For details about the *Chickens* arrangements, see Sittig, 'L. Prang & Company,' 70–71. Sittig notes that 'Many of [Prang's chromos] listed in the 1870 catalogue were still available in 1894' (59). Cadbury gives further information on Prang's dealings with Tait, 77–85, and includes a checklist based on Tait's notebooks by Henry F. Marsh. It also provides helpful information, including Tait's notes on the terms of the sale of his *Ducklings* (1866) and *Quails* to Prang: 'L. Prang. (Boston) for publication. I am to receive 10 per cent of the gross receipts of all sales of the prints' (193).

19. Lillian B. Miller, *Patron and Patriotism; the Encouragement of the Fine Arts in the United States, 1790–1860* (Chicago: University of Chicago Press, 1966), 33–84, discusses artists' hopes and disappointments in seeking support for their efforts from the federal government.

Collaborative mass production, rather than individual crafting of unique objects, became the dominant form. This of course was not a change that Prang brought about single-handedly or completely, but it is an example of how commercial mass culture emerged. (By 'commercial' I mean that monetary gain was the primary motivation; by 'mass' I am indicating industrial production of identical objects in large quantities for widespread distribution and consumption.) The Prang company (and chromolithographic publishing in general) brought about a dramatic increase in the number of people who had daily experience with art, and a notable broadening of the range of objects considered art to include multiples reproduced by machine as well as unique handcrafted objects.[20]

L. Prang and Co.'s promotion of the arts came from a particular perspective that differed from other art institutions. Prang was not primarily interested in securing patronage or markets for artists' works. He was concerned with serving the art-consuming public. Toward the end of his career Prang congratulated himself: 'I have succeeded to raise the standard of popular production to the highest point possible to our art and to elevate thereby public taste and public appreciation for the beautiful.'[21] Successful in achieving his goal of disseminating art, Prang's wealth increased, since he made money rather than spending it as an art promoter/businessman.

Through chromolithography, paintings became a reproducible commodity, while expanding their cultural power as an educative force. By then, the means and purposes of art education through art had shifted. John Gadsby Chapman's *The American Drawing Book*, a drawing manual popular for decades after its first publication in 1847, outlined a program for self-education in basic art

---

20. This process had begun at least as early as the widespread distribution of woodcuts and engravings in the fifteenth and sixteenth centuries. Chromolithography, however, added greatly to the technical sophistication, cheapness, and sheer number of images that could be reproduced.

21. 'Autobiography of Louis Prang' in Sittig, 'L. Prang & Company,' 154.

FROM NATURE. 185

24

Fig. 5. Examples from John Gadsby Chapman's *The Amercian Drawing Book* (New York: J. S. Redfield, 1847), 185. American Antiquarian Society.

skills through diligent practice in drawing from nature (fig. 5). Prang and his supporters advocated a more passive form of art education—art to be looked at, chromolithographs. The benefits art brought also changed. Rather than teaching a skill which could help one on the way to becoming a professional artist or at least a more refined and appreciative amateur, Prang's prints taught domestic and civic virtues through didactic images. As the Beecher sisters declared in 1869: 'The educating influence of these works of art can hardly be over-estimated. Surrounded by such suggestions of the beautiful, and such reminders of history and art, children are constantly trained to correctness of taste and refinement of thought.'[22] Art here imparts moral lessons to casual observers, especially children, rather than emphasizing the development of artistic skills by diligent students.

In addition to making art reproductions, Prang also contributed to practical training in the arts. After the Civil War there were new needs in art education, including a pressing demand for designers and skilled mechanics in industry.[23] A large percentage of the value of furniture, building components, ceramics, and other common goods was added by the artistry of their design. Because of the shortage of skilled designers and workers many manufactured items had to be imported, chiefly from Europe. This not only hurt the domestic economy, it was a disappointing indication to cultural nationalists that the United States was not yet free of its apprenticeship to European standards and abilities.[24]

Prang was a resident of Massachusetts, a state which was a national leader in public education. In 1870 the legislature pushed a

22. Catharine E. Beecher and Harriet Beecher Stowe, *The American Woman's Home* (New York: J. B. Ford and Company, 1869), 93–94.

23. On the need for a new sort of art education, see Diana Korzenik, *Drawn to Art; A Nineteenth-Century American Dream* (Hanover, N.H.: University Press of New England, 1985), 22–25 and 218–20. Korzenik explains that the new form of art education aimed at creating 'skilled art labor' (23) for industrial production. She also discusses the motivations which drove people to acquire such skills. Because of the cultural link forged between art and industry, art skills, particularly drawing, promised employment as well as more elusive satisfactions.

24. In addition to being elaborated by Smith, these difficulties and imperatives were noted at length in governmental considerations and reports such as Isaac Edwards Clarke, *Art and Industry. Education in the Industrial and Fine Arts in the United States. Part 1; Drawing in Public Schools* (Washington: Government Printing Office, 1885). The 1876 Centennial in Philadelphia was a crucial motivator for both individuals and government agencies. As Clarke stated: 'The great awakening of the people to the value of taste as an element of manufactures and to a knowledge of the many possible applications of art to industrial products, which came from a sight of the displays made of foreign wares and tissues at the Centennial Exposition, has led to general interest in all forms of art training which promise practical results in similar productions in our own country' (5).

Fig. 6. Louis Prang, *Slate Pictures; A Drawing School for Beginners* (1863), 4–5. American Antiquarian Society.

step further by requiring all public schools to teach drawing and all towns of over 10,000 inhabitants to offer free evening classes in industrial drawing for adults. The state also aimed to set up a system of normal schools to train art teachers. All of this activity was under the direction of the state director of art education, Walter Smith, a man recruited from England for the job. He had had experience in the successful British system of industrial art schools, whose main facility was at South Kensington. Smith was a strong believer in the practical and economic value of artworks and art skills, tying art training directly to increased worker productivity.[25]

25. Walter Smith was a convincing spokesman and prolific writer on behalf of his ideas about the importance of art education. See, for example, his *Art Education, Scholastic and Industrial* (Boston: James R. Osgood and Company, 1873). On Smith and his appointment, see Korzenik, *Drawn to Art*, 153–59.

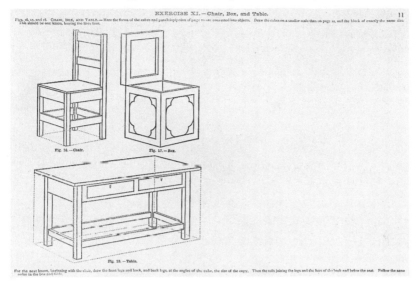

EXERCISE XI.—Chair, Box, and Table.

Figs. 16, 17, and 18. CHAIR, BOX, AND TABLE.— Here the forms of the cubes and parallelopipedon of page 10 are converted into objects. Draw the cubes on a smaller scale than on page 10, and the block of exactly the same size. This should be one lesson, leaving the lines faint.

Fig. 16.—Chair.   Fig. 17.—Box.

Fig. 18.—Table.

For the next lesson, beginning with the chair, draw the front legs and back, and back legs, at the angles of the cube, the size of the copy. Then the rails joining the legs and the bars of the back and below the seat. Follow the same order in the box and table.

Fig. 7. Walter Smith, *American Text Books of Art Education, Intermediate Course, Number 3,* 'Exercise XI—Chair, Box, and Table.' American Antiquarian Society.

Prang had long been interested in practical art education. As early as 1863 he published an exercise book called *Slate Pictures; Drawing School for Beginners.* This was a series of white line drawings on a black ground imitating chalk drawings on a blackboard (thus the title) to be used as models by students (fig. 6). Among the projects Prang executed in association with Smith were the so-called 'Smith Books.'[26] This was a series of graduated lessons designed to allow teachers to impart mastery of the fundamentals of drawing in three year-long courses (fig. 7). The Smith books continued to uphold Chapman's celebrated claim that 'Any one who can learn to write can learn to draw,' but they emphasized the application of drawing skills in industry and trades rather than preparation for continued training as a fine artist. In terms of

26. *American Text Books of Art Education* (Boston: James R. Osgood, 1873, 1874, and Louis Prang and Co., 1875). Korzenik discusses the mutually beneficial cooperation between Smith and Prang, *Drawn to Art,* 160–65 and 196–97.

moral lessons too, the goals of art education shifted to address a different class of people and different social requirements, shifted from refinement and development of artistic genius to self-discipline and useful skills. The subject matter and methods emphasized suggest the nature of the change. Whereas Chapman had focused on drawing from nature, with rendering of the human figure as a goal, *Slate Pictures* and the Smith books were based on copying examples from books, usually schematic images of regular, manufactured objects or abstractions from natural forms which could serve as decoration for commercial wares.[27]

Prang took part in two quite different kinds of art education. On the one hand, his interest in edifying a large audience by placing art reproductions within their reach made Prang a leader in the movement to popularize art. Prang's audience consisted mostly of members of the middle class who, whatever their knowledge of art, were aware of the enlightened and enlightening cachet of art. This large audience was not composed primarily of artists, even amateur artists, or of knowledgeable connoisseurs. On the other hand, Prang was heavily involved in a more active, participatory kind of art education, training in basic art skills that could be applied to a variety of occupations besides that of artist.

This division of art education was a departure from more integrated notions of art education such as those Chapman presented in *The American Drawing Book*. Whereas Chapman offered the same program and purposes to amateurs and to artists working in fine and applied arts, Prang served three distinct groups, each in a different way. For a wide audience of buyers, he produced relatively inexpensive art reproductions. For aspiring students and industrial workers, he published reference books and instructional manuals. To the practicing fine artist, he gave modest patronage.

A major effect of the movement towards mass culture in which Prang participated was the integration of art into mainstream American culture and into the daily experience of a broad public.

27. On drawing manuals, see Peter C. Marzio, *The Art Crusade: An Analysis of American Drawing Manuals, 1820–1860* (Washington, D.C.: Smithsonian Institution Press, 1976).

This integration was accomplished only when older ideas of art's educating, refining, uplifting function were melded with industrial capabilities and objectives. This was not a straightforward triumph for the fine arts, but instead the creation of a new hybrid between commercial art and popular culture whose development continues even now.[28]

Art entrepreneurs like Prang entered a whole new realm of opportunities. Mass production and the ability to buy art services as labor created immense profit potential. Prang's company was one model of a reorganization of the art market, relying on the specialization of labor, collaborative creative efforts, corporate business structure, and mass marketing. By using these tools, Prang moved toward making art a reproducible commodity in an industrialized marketplace. In the process, he helped to change prevailing understandings of both what art was and what role art could play in shaping productive and creative capacities.[29]

Artists, however, were not demonstrably better off with the coming of the mass reproduction of artworks. Rather than solving the nagging question of how artists could gain adequate support and encouragement, mass reproduction provided a hugely successful alternative to museum and gallery venues. Fine artists saw little of the profits of this achievement, and would have cause to complain of general neglect well into the twentieth century. Commercial artists faced an unstable future as technical innovations threatened to make their skills obsolete.[30] Commercial mass culture created many new opportunities, but business people, not artists, were the major beneficiaries.

28. In the upper strata of the art market, the trend after the Civil War was away from support of American artists toward an interest in the more polished, expensive, and traditionally prestigious productions of European salons. On these developments, see Linda Henefield Skalet, 'The Market for American Painting in New York, 1870–1915' (Ph.D. diss., Johns Hopkins University, 1980).

29. Michele H. Bogart describes a later stage in the use of artistic talent within commercial mass culture and the opportunities and dilemmas it created for artists in 'Artistic Ideals and Commercial Practices: The Problem of Status for American Illustrators,' *Prospects* 15 (1990): 225–81.

30. Korzenik, *Drawn to Art*, 247–55, discusses the disappointment and disillusionment at the end of the nineteenth century of a generation of artists who had been attracted to commercial art as a lucrative and rewarding career.

Quiet Pleasures

SINCLAIR HITCHINGS

Bruce Chandler is a designer, draftsman, watercolorist, etcher, lithographer, wood engraver, and letterpress printer—a versatile artist and craftsman who from time to time chooses texts, and designs, sets type, illustrates, and prints those texts as limited-edition books of his Heron Press.

When he engraves on wood, he works in a medium easily accessible to all of us. Many years ago, Mark McCorison and I made a pilgrimage to Northampton to visit Leonard Baskin. The three of us sat and talked around the Baskin's kitchen table. In his left hand, Baskin held a small woodblock; cradled in his right hand, with the curved end of the wooden handle backed against his palm, he held a burin. From time to time, he would pause in his talk, survey the surface of the block, and engrave another line or two. He would tilt the block until the engraved surface caught the light and he could see how his intended design was coming along. There was a relaxed, intimate, domestic feeling to this kitchen-table session of conversation and wood engraving. The medium of wood engraving lends itself to such scenes.

My own initiation into the medium came in Ray Nash's Graphic Arts Workshop at Dartmouth College. Professor Nash liked woodcuts and wood engravings not only for the opportunities they offer for simple, bold designs in black and white, but also for the fact that woodblocks can be type-high and can be locked up with handset type to produce a broadside or folder or small pamphlet—an ideal experience for students learning about book de-

---

SINCLAIR HITCHINGS is keeper of prints at Boston Public Library.

139

sign, illustration, and printing. I am not an artist, and after my first lessons in wood engraving, I chose for my subjects several birds; some of the outlines I traced from Roger Tory Peterson's illustrations of American birds in his field guides. I went to a couple of lumber yards and inquired about woods which might be suitable. I asked for waste pieces, leftovers from cuttings; I inquired for apple, pear, and cherry, and ended up with several pieces of mahogany. My occasional student efforts as a wood engraver continued probably for a year and left me with a lasting sense of the attractions of this medium of picture-making.

Tonight, Bruce Chandler has brought woodblocks and tools for wood engraving. He will talk to us about this skill.

The Imp of the Reverse

BRUCE CHANDLER

ART of what I find exciting about a wood engraving or
woodcut is the pulling of the first proof. Not only is it the
first time I am able to see on paper what I have been cutting into the wood, but the impression is completely in reverse.
Now I must reenter and familiarize myself once again with the
dynamic of the image.

A wood engraving begins with a sketch that is either transferred
or drawn directly onto the surface of a highly polished piece of
end-grain boxwood. In earlier times, when large wood engravings
were produced commercially for magazines and newspapers, the
image was transferred by hand or photomechanically to a woodblock made up of mortised sections. The sections were then un-
fastened, and each was given to a different professional engraver
who would, usually unerringly, engrave the design on that surface.
After the engraving was finished, the individual sections were
gathered and rejoined, corrected, proofed, and printed. Today,
most artists who use the medium create their own images and cut
the blocks themselves.

When a drawing is transferred, the cutting and engraving begins.
The block is usually placed on a sand-filled leather pad or 'mound'
for mobility in executing curved lines (by spinning the block).
The engraver will be looking at his work through magnifiers—
either a mounted glass, or a jeweller's visor, which I prefer.

The usual method of engraving on wood is similar to that of a

BRUCE CHANDLER is a printmaker, printer, and proprietor of
The Heron Press in Boston.

woodcut, in that the wood is cut away from the lines or shapes that will be positively printed and read. Albrecht Dürer's woodcuts are excellent examples. Thomas Bewick, an early nineteenth-century English artist, was the pioneer of *white*-line wood engraving. Alexander Anderson, who admired Bewick's little prints, introduced the technique to the United States. Early in the twentieth century, Timothy Cole became an American virtuoso of the technique. Though it is not used as much today, artists including Thomas Nason and Asa Cheffetz, and later, George Lockwood, have been practitioners as recently as the 1960s. The artist cuts away the wood to make a positive white mark, almost like drawing with white chalk on a blackboard. The beauty of this method can be imagined, with all gradations from pure white to solid black being achieved.

As the engraver works his tools, which have names like lozenge, elliptical tint tool, scorper, and spitsticker, all of them creating their own mark and performing a specific function, he rubs talcum powder into the engraved lines, creating a contrast between the drawn image and the wood, enabling him to see his work clearly. Finally, a point is reached when before cutting and forming the image any further, a reversed image must be seen. A proof must be pulled. The surface of the block is rolled with ink, a piece of soft proofing paper selected, and the proof made, either by placing the paper over the inked block and burnishing the paper surface with a wooden spoon or tool-handle, or by placing the inked block onto the bed of a printing press and pulling a proof mechanically.

And there it is, a newborn image in reverse: never quite as originally envisioned, but filled with new expectation and surprise. And now the work begins again.

The Graver, the Brush, and the Ruling Machine: The Training of Late-Nineteenth-Century Wood Engravers

ANN PRENTICE WAGNER

INSLOW HOMER'S illustrations of American life, Thomas Nast's political cartoons, and many other images emblematic of nineteenth-century America originally reached the world through the efforts of wood engravers. Wood engraving was the predominant medium used to reproduce illustrations in books, magazines, and newspapers during the mid to late nineteenth century, and there was a high demand for skilled practitioners of the art.[1] Legions of young men and women who dreamed of lives as fine artists recognized the economic uncertainties of such a life and instead sought training in wood engraving. The numerous illustration firms and illus-

I would like to thank the following people for their help with this article: Helena E. Wright, Curator of Graphic Arts, National Museum of American Art; Sinclair Hitchings, Keeper of Prints, Boston Public Library, and Karen Shafts, his assistant; Georgia B. Barnhill, the Andrew W. Mellon Curator of Graphic Arts, American Antiquarian Society; Paul Ritscher, wood engraver and collector of materials related to the history of wood engraving; and my parents, John and Polly Wagner.

1. Frank Weitenkampf, *American Graphic Art* (New York: Henry Holt and Co., 1912), 120–21.

ANN PRENTICE WAGNER is curatorial assistant and collections manager of the Department of Prints and Drawings of the National Portrait Gallery, Smithsonian Institution. Her book *Hiram Merrill: Memories of a Wood Engraver* is being published by the Boston Public Library.

trated magazines in New York, Boston, Chicago, Philadelphia, and other cities employed hundreds of engravers, but only until the mid 1890s when photographic processes of reproduction largely replaced wood engraving.

Before the perfection of such photographic processes as halftone and line block, wood engraving was the reproduction process best suited to the needs of illustration because it produced a relief printing block which was the same height as letterpress type. This block was printed simultaneously with the text using the same press. Lithography and metal engraving were also used to reproduce illustrations, but were less practical because they required the use of one kind of press for the illustrations and another for the text.

A wood engraving was a relief print made from a very hard, fine-grained block of boxwood cut across the grain, rather than parallel to the grain as in a woodcut. Since boxwood comes only in very small sections, printing blocks were usually made from multiple pieces bolted, dowelled, or glued together. The engraver cut into the surface of the block to remove the areas which would not print. He used a narrow, sharpened metal rod called a graver, similar to the burin used in metal engravings. The graver cut fine white lines and its point made tiny white triangles for stippling. When the engraver finished work on the block a metal casting called an electrotype was made from it. The electrotype was printed along with the text on the page.

The engraver himself seldom drew the original illustration to be reproduced. His work was purely reproductive and for this reason illustrators and fine artists tended to regard him as a common, insensitive workman. An illustrator made the original illustration, a more or less finished drawing which he or another artist, known as a designer on wood, copied onto the surface of the boxwood block using pencil, India ink washes, and Chinese white watercolor.[2]

2. Nancy Carlson Schrock, introduction to *American Wood Engraving: A Victorian History*, by William J. Linton (Watkins Glen, N. Y.: Published for the Athenaeum Library of Nineteenth Century America by The American Life Foundation & Study Institute, 1976), 1.

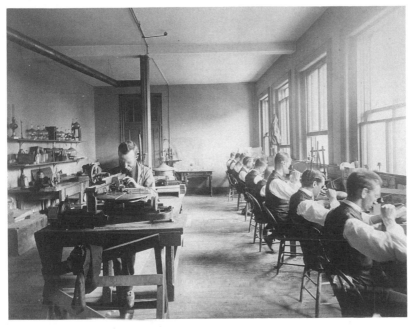

Fig. 1. Russell & Richardson, Engravers on Wood, Temple Place, Boston. Undated photograph. Courtesy of the Division of Graphic Arts, National Museum of American History.

The unique drawing on the wood was destroyed as the engraver worked, making corrections very difficult. The engraver cut out the white areas around black lines and interpreted grey tones of the drawing into a network of white lines or dots. He employed a ruling machine as an aid in engraving large fields of parallel straight or wavy lines representing grey tones.[3] A wood engraver is using a ruling machine at the left in figure 1.

Later in the century art to be engraved could be transferred to the block photographically. Patents for processes of photography on wood were granted to Robert Price in 1857 and to C. B. Boyle in 1859, but it was several years before these processes were widely

3. David M. Sander, *Wood Engraving: An Adventure in Printmaking* (New York: Viking Press), 21–22.

used.[4] Photography on wood allowed the engraver to use the
original art or a separate photograph of it for a guide while he
worked (fig. 2). This technology could transfer any kind of art
onto a block, which meant that the engraver often had to trans-
late the tones of a photograph, oil painting, or watercolor into
white lines and dots.[5]

In 1877 engravers working for *Scribner's Monthly* (which became *Century Magazine* in 1881) and *Harper's Monthly* magazines
began to put increased emphasis on tone and texture rather than
line in interpreting the brush strokes of paintings and the grey
tones of photographs.[6] They created a variety of intricate effects
using the previously spurned techniques of white dot stipple and
cross hatching with white lines to make fields of fine black
lozenges. Such rising young masters of the craft as Timothy Cole
(1852–1930), Frederick Juengling (1846–84), and John G.
Smithwick (fl. 1870s–80s) worked with the narrowest of tools to
reproduce the effects of the original art. They and their followers
were known as the New School, in contrast to the linear Old
School. At first glance, some of their illustrations hardly strike the
viewer as relief prints. Their lines and dots can be so fine as to
read almost as continuous grey tones rather than the marks of a
graver.

Alexander W. Drake, art superintendent of *Century Magazine*
from 1881 to 1912, was a major advocate of the New School.[7] In
1883 Timothy Cole went to Europe to make wood engravings for
Century directly from Old Master paintings. The *Century's* readers received Cole's virtuoso engravings with tremendous acclaim.
Cole remained in Europe until 1910, then engraved paintings
from American collections for several years, continuing to make
wood engravings long after they ceased to be the most widely

4. Robert Taft, *Photography and the American Scene: Social History* (New York: Mac-
millan, 1942), 422–23.
5. George Howes Whittle, 'The Swan Song of Wood Engraving,' *The Printing Art* 34
(January 1920): 392.
6. Weitenkampf, *American Graphic Art*, 126–28.
7. Peter Hastings Falk, ed., *Who Was Who in American Art* (Madison, Conn.: Sound
View Press, 1985), 172.

Fig. 2. W. Klasen of *Harper's* engraves a block, consulting a reference photograph of the art he is reproducing. Undated photograph. Hiram C. Merrill Collection, Boston Public Library.

used form of reproduction.[8] Before practical methods of photo-reproduction and convenient travel, the reading public was thrilled to be able to see high-quality reproductions of otherwise inaccessible great art.

In the 1860s, 1870s, and 1880s wood engraving looked like a very promising field for a young person to enter. By 1870 there were about 400 wood engravers employed in the United States, and the number increased rapidly.[9] For those seeking to enter the world of art without expensive academic education, this industry offered training that led to dependable employment in a field intimately related to art. The expansion of publication and illustration in the United States in the middle of the nineteenth century provided plenty of picture books and illustrated magazines to inspire children with ideas of art and illustration. Those inclined to art found a ready supply of wood-engraved illustrations to study and to copy. The industrially-oriented drawing classes taught in Massachusetts public schools and other school systems that emulated them also encouraged numerous young people to look to art as a possible career.[10]

People wanting to learn wood engraving might find instruction in manuals like William A. Emerson's *Hand-Book of Wood Engraving with Practical Instruction in the Art for Persons Wishing to Learn Without an Instructor* (1881). Although Emerson thought that prospective professionals might use his manual, he admitted that 'It is not reasonable to suppose that a book of this kind, however full and complete, will take the place of a good teacher.' The introduction to the second edition states that the first edition had been received with favor by amateurs.[11] Such manuals did not seem to play a significant part in the training of professional wood engravers.

8. Alphaeus P. Cole and Margaret Ward Cole, *Timothy Cole: Wood-Engraver* (New York: The Pioneer Associates, 1935), 36, 141–55.

9. Sue Rainey, *Creating 'Picturesque America': Monument to the Natural and Cultural Landscape* (Nashville, Tenn.: Vanderbilt University Press, 1994), 179, 349.

10. Diana Korzenik, *Drawn to Art: A Nineteenth-Century American Dream* (Hanover, N.H.: University Press of New England, 1985), 153–54.

11. William A. Emerson, *Handbook of Wood Engraving* (Boston: Lee & Shepard, 1881), 7–8.

In his wood engraving manual of 1890 William Norman Brown described a group considered well suited to be professional wood engravers: 'refined women who from various causes, compelled to battle with the world alone, have turned to some one or other artistic pursuit for the means of earning an honourable and respectable livelihood.'[12] Sarah E. Fuller (c. 1829–1901), who engraved for *Harper's* and other magazines, wrote a manual on wood engraving in 1867 in which she urged women to become professional wood engravers.[13]

The majority of wood engravers, however, were male. An apprenticeship of four to seven years was the normal method of training for male wood engravers, but some had shorter apprenticeships. Timothy Cole's training began almost by accident. Young Cole had always loved to draw, so his father, who loved big words and was enchanted by the word lithographer, planned to apprentice him to a lithographer. On the morning when the father was taking his son to begin his apprenticeship in a lithography shop in Chicago, the pair happened to see the wood engraving shop of Bond & Chandler. Cole's father asked his son if he would like to be a wood engraver. When Cole answered positively, the boy was promptly apprenticed for seven years. Cole served only two years of his time, for when the great Chicago Fire interrupted his studies in 1871, he had already mastered the art of engraving.[14]

Although William B. Closson (1848–1926) began by teaching himself how to engrave, he had to serve some time as an apprentice before his work reached a professional standard. Closson conducted his self-instruction while working as a railroad clerk. He got up at four o'clock every morning to practice by copying illustrations he had seen. On entering a Boston wood engraving

12. William Norman Brown, *Wood Engraving: A Practical and Easy Introduction to a Study of the Art* (London: C. Lockwood, 1890), v.

13. Fuller, S. E., *A Manual of Instruction in the Art of Wood Engraving* (Boston: Joseph Watson, 1867), iii–iv; Chris Petteys, *Dictionary of Women Artists, An International Dictionary of Women Artists Born Before 1900* (Boston: G. K. Hall & Co., 1985), 266.

14. Cole and Cole, *Timothy Cole*, 5–6, 9–10.

firm, Closson began his apprenticeship at the salary usually paid to second-year apprentices.[15]

Elbridge Kingsley (1841–1918), a wood engraver famed for the refinement of his work interpreting paintings, began work in New York as a typesetter with J. W. Orr's illustration firm. Orr's was one of many shops that contracted to provide illustrations for books, magazines, newspapers, advertisements, broadsides, product labels, and catalogues. Kingsley had drawn and painted since he was a child and was interested in moving into a career concerned with art. He recalled in his autobiography: 'I think here I was in a wavering state of mind. Many young men were going abroad to study Art, and somehow I thought I could do it as well as another. But somehow the acquaintances that I made had no faith in Art as a means of getting a living, and so finally I got into the Engraving Rooms as the safest way to support myself and perhaps study Art too.' So in 1863 Kingsley became an apprentice wood engraver for J. W. Orr.[16]

Such a shop is seen in figure 1, a photograph of Russell & Richardson, Engravers on Wood, Temple Place, Boston. The engravers are shown working at a row of desks next to a row of windows, utilizing natural light filtered through paper shades. At night, gas lamps provided light that was focused by the water-filled globes seen on the shelves at the far left. The engravers used magnifying lenses to reduce the strain on their eyes.

Hiram Merrill (1866–1958), a wood engraver whose life is well documented in the Hiram Campbell Merrill Collection of the Boston Public Library, began his career in the typical fashion with an apprenticeship of several years in an illustration firm. Two major factors urged Merrill, like so many young people in the late nineteenth century, toward a career in wood engraving: he was poor and he was interested in art. His father was a wheelwright

15. George Howes Whittle, 'Monographs on American Wood Engravers,' *The Printing Art* 31 (April 1918): 118.
16. Elbridge Kingsley, 'Life and Works of Elbridge Kingsley, Painter-Engraver,' Northampton, Mass.: Forbes Library; Washington, D.C.: microfilm roll #48 in Archives of American Art, Smithsonian Institution), 32–33.

and, as the family probably had no connection to art, Merrill is unlikely to have received any particular encouragement in that direction. Despite this, from an early age he drew from nature and dreamed of being a painter.[17] Merrill attended drawing classes at Shepard Grammar School in Cambridge, Massachusetts, and a surviving report card records that he received excellent grades in drawing.[18] Merrill summed up his situation: 'The necessity to earn money decided me to embrace wood engraving, as I was told it was lucrative.'[19]

In 1882 he began an apprenticeship in the shop of John Andrew and Son. This shop on the corner of Temple Place and Tremont Street, Boston, specialized in fine book illustration. Merrill recorded that when he entered the shop 'An apprenticeship of four years was agreed on: two dollars a week for the first year; three dollars the next year; then four dollars; and, finally, five or six dollars, according to my ability. I am happy to say I got that six dollars.'[20]

New apprentices spent much of their time running errands, cleaning the shop, and stealing moments on the side to practice cutting lines on boxwood. Occasionally Grottenthaler, a boxwood dealer in Boston, would give apprentices like Merrill small pieces of wood for practice.[21] Even though Edward Howard Del'Orme was the son of a wood engraver, he had to save his pennies to buy his own practice blocks and to get art photographed onto them.[22]

It took a long time for a beginner to learn to control his graver. For Elbridge Kingsley 'the mechanical training in engraving was never easy. . . . I know it was some time before I could cut a clean

17. Hiram Campbell Merrill, *Wood Engraving and Wood Engravers* (Boston: Society of Printers, 1937), 4.

18. Report card in the Hiram Campbell Merrill Collection of the Boston Public Library.

19. Merrill, *Wood Engraving and Wood Engravers*, 4.

20. *Ibid.*

21. Hiram Merrill manuscript notes in Hiram Campbell Merrill Collection of the Boston Public Library.

22. George Howes Whittle, 'Monographs on American Wood Engravers,' *The Printing Art* 31 (August 1918): 429.

Fig. 3. *Chateau Chillon, Lake Geneva, Switzerland,* wood engraving by Hiram Merrill after unknown original, 1882. Merrill's first wood engraving made while he was an apprentice. Hiram C. Merrill Collection, Boston Public Library.

line or finish a reliable transfer. . . . A beginner's work is usually fac-similie [*sic*], made up of lines drawn or transferred on the block [instead of grey tones which practiced wood engravers could interpret into lines]. The student is required to cut these lines sharp and clean so as to print as well as the original copy. . . . I did gradually conquer the fac-similie stage and was able to be of some use, and then slowly came the ability to make light and shade by the means of line and picks [by stipple made with the end of a graver].'[23]

In Merrill's very first wood engraving (fig. 3), made in 1882, we can see a beginner learning to describe simple shapes with tints made of parallel lines. As a manual observed, 'It is not probable that the learner will succeed in keeping the tool from going upward, thus making the line thinner, or downward, making it thicker; but by following the directions closely he may succeed in making a fair line.'[24] Figure 4 shows a vastly more polished illustration made just four years later by the same engraver at the end of his apprenticeship.

Busy at their blocks, veterans seldom took time to instruct the

23. Kingsley, 'Life and Works,' 33.
24. Emerson, *Handbook*, 54–55.

Fig. 4. 'Australian Landscape,' wood engraving by Hiram Merrill after Frederick B. Schell, c. 1886. Illustration made for *Cassell's Picturesque Australasia*, by Edward Ellis Morris (New York: Cassell & Co., 1887). Reproduced in *Wood Engraving and Wood Engravers*, by Hiram C. Merrill (Boston: Society of Printers, 1937). Hiram C. Merrill Collection, Boston Public Library.

apprentices. The best instruction came from observing the work done by the experienced engravers. Elbridge Kingsley described how 'The beginners were glad of a glimpse of the work of the older men while they were at dinner. In fact this was one of the ways to get on and acquire judgement in textures. And the advent of a new man was an especial chance to make comparisons. I remember the first appearance of John Minton at our office. He was noted for the purity of his line, and we could hardly wait for him to go out before examining his work. He cut a more refined line than any of our force, the only trouble with him being that he might be off on a spree before finishing the work in hand.'[25]

This close observation caused certain stylistic traits to become characteristic of a particular shop. Hiram Merrill recalled that 'A wavy line, dating back to [Thomas] Bewick's time [the eighteenth century] or earlier, was too often used by the engravers in John

25. Kingsley, 'Life and Works,' 36–37.

Andrew & Son's engraving shop. . . . It was called "Andrew's wiggle" by those inclined to be critical.'[26] Andrew's wiggle may be seen in patches of shading in Merrill's engraving of an Australian landscape (fig. 4).

Apprentices also learned by collecting examples of wood engraving by various masters. According to Kingsley, 'Some apprentices were great collectors of prints, and eagerly discussed anything new.'[27] George Howes Whittle noted that 'The young engravers . . . were enthusiastic in collecting prints of wood engraving from current publications both American and foreign. The *Illustrated London News* and other English and French publications furnished interesting and instructive examples of the work of the period. Earlier engravings were sought for the boys' scrapbooks and were highly prized and jealously guarded as potent influences and guides in the formation of their style.'[28]

New stylistic ideas passed from wood engraver to wood engraver at John C. Bauer's New York City printing shop at 10 North William Street, where many engravers had their works proofed. Merrill recalled that 'here the engravers met and had many a warm discussion on the merits of this and that type of line, and working conditions in general.'[29] Kingsley called Bauer's shop 'the center . . . for the New School.'[30] While many artists, engravers, art editors, and the public enthusiastically embraced the New School, a small but vocal group protested against the abandonment of pure line and the effacement of the engraver's personal style of interpretation. Led by the British immigrant William J. Linton (1812–97), leader of the Old School, they scorned the New School engraver's imitation of other forms of art, even the imitation of brush strokes, as a blasphemous betrayal of the character of the wood.[31]

26. Merrill manuscript notes, Merrill Collection.

27. Kingsley, 'Life and Works,' 35.

28. George Howes Whittle, 'Monographs on American Wood Engravers,' *The Printing Art* 31 (April 1918): 118.

29. Merrill manuscript notes, Merrill Collection.

30. Kingsley, 'Life and Works,' 45, 84–85.

31. William James Linton, *The History of Wood Engraving in America* (Boston: Estes and

Some veteran engravers occasionally took time to instruct and encourage the apprentices and younger engravers. The engravers in the Andrew and Son shop chipped in to buy a set of tools for Merrill as a Christmas present his first year as an apprentice.[32] When Kingsley grew skilled enough to take part in the work in J. W. Orr's shop, he shared his desk with the older engravers John Minton and Phineas F. Annin. Kingsley commented that 'Both were generous by nature, and kind in helping along younger men. Annin would take my block and work a little on it; just to give me a hint.'[33]

Henry Herrick, who was also an illustrator and a fine artist, was one of the established wood engravers who acted as mentors to younger people in the field. During his frequent visits to his parents in Manchester, New Hampshire, Herrick met young Henry Clay Cross and Joel Foster Cross, sons of a local farmer. Herrick soon realized the interest these children and their sister had in art and encouraged them to draw. He became a close friend of the Cross family and taught the boys the skills that enabled them to become professional wood engravers.[34] Later, when Herrick moved permanently to Manchester, his son became friends with his schoolmate Stephen Greeley Putnam. Putnam visited the elder Herrick's painting and engraving studio, where the boy saw many fine wood engravings and illustrated books. When Putnam was old enough to consider a career, he returned to Henry Herrick's studio to learn wood engraving.

Putnam gained his first engraving job through the aid of Frank French.[35] French was a New Hampshire farm boy who had learned about the profitable possibilities of wood engraving from an advertisement in *Scribner's Magazine*. Henry Herrick's protégé Foster Cross helped French to select blocks and tools and in-

Lauriat, 1882); facsimile edition reprinted as *American Wood Engraving, A Victorian History* (Watkins Glen, N.Y.: Published for the Athenaeum Library of Nineteenth Century America by the American Life Foundation & Study Institute, 1976), 45–71.

32. Merrill, *Wood Engraving and Wood Engravers*, 4.

33. Kingsley, 'Life and Works,' 41.

34. Korzenik, *Drawn to Art*, 31–33, 57, 60, 64, 67–69, 87, 100, 108–10, 124.

35. George Howes Whittle, 'Monographs on American Wood Engravers,' *The Printing Art* 32 (November 1918): 169–72.

structed him in how to use them. French received further instruction from Henry Herrick himself. He next went to work for
the American Tract Society, a publishing firm in New York City.[36]
Elias J. Whitney, superintendent of engraving for the Tract
Society, further trained and encouraged French. Whitney taught
many young engravers including his own younger brother, John
H. E. Whitney.[37]

A doctor who had once been a wood engraver guided Frederick
A. Pettit in the direction of wood engraving after the young man
injured his hip so seriously that he could not continue his work on
a farm.[38] Wood engraving was considered a suitable career for
those unable to do heavy work. The great New School wood engraver Timothy Cole trained several disabled people to engrave
in the informal wood engraving school he ran in the tower studio
of his Long Island home.[39]

Many engravers, Cole and Kingsley among them, began working with firms that specialized in catalogue illustration and illustrations of machinery.[40] This work, while cold and mechanical in
appearance and dull for the engraver, provided good discipline for
a young engraver. Emerson's engraving manual emphasized that
such machinery as stoves required absolutely perfect drawing in
perspective. The least distortion in rendering a round lid on a
stove top would make the metal look warped.[41] A ruling machine
was vital for the precise parallel lines needed to describe machinery and architecture.[42]

Merrill's apprenticeship with a firm that did book illustration—among the finest and most artistic of the many varieties of
wood engraving—was unusual. After a young engraver had mas-

36. George Howes Whittle, 'Monographs on American Wood Engravers,' *The Printing Art* 31 (March 1918): 37.

37. George Howes Whittle, 'Monographs on American Wood Engravers,' *The Printing Art* 30 (October 1917): 88.

38. George Howes Whittle, 'Monographs on American Wood Engravers,' *The Printing Art* 32 (February 1919): 397.

39. Cole and Cole, *Timothy Cole: Wood Engraver*, 21, 26.

40. *Ibid.*, 6; Kingsley, 'Life and Works,' 34.

41. Emerson, *Handbook*, 81.

42. Sander, *Wood Engraving*, 21.

tered more straightforward work he would move on to the more artistic areas of illustration for newspapers, school books, magazines, and fine books. Figure 4, an illustration engraved by Merrill after a drawing by Frederick B. Schell for *Cassell's Picturesque Australasia* is an example of such fine illustration work. This book, like many others, was inspired by the great success of the lavishly illustrated *Picturesque America*, published by Appleton and Company starting in 1872.[43] Illustrated book engravers took their time engraving such illustrations. Merrill said, 'Work was leisurely done, a half day often being spent on planning ways to engrave an important subject—the size, direction, and varieties of line to use in interpreting it.'[44]

In 1890 Merrill moved to New York City because he felt that 'the New York magazines seemed a wider field for advancement, and I was then engraving on the best class of Andrew's work.'[45] He found a job with *Harper's*, the great magazine publishing firm, where he found quite a different routine. The engravers were constantly working on the relatively fine and deliberate illustrations for the small format *Monthly*, but when the much larger pages of the *Weekly* required a large illustration, there was no time to lose. The illustrations for the *Weekly* were drawn in a coarser style than those for the *Monthly* and could be more quickly engraved, but the pressure of a weekly deadline made it impossible for one man to engrave a single or double page illustration spread in time. The blocks would be split into eight or more pieces and each piece would be given to a different engraver to be finished overnight. Merrill recounted the routine.

> When a rush page for the *Weekly* was wanted, Mr. Smithwick (the director) would come around about three o'clock and whisper: 'We're going to be busy tonight, Merrill, so you had better go out and get the air. Be back by 6 o'clock!'
> I would promptly head for Dietz's Weinstube, which was crowded

43. Albert F. Moritz, *America the Picturesque in Nineteenth Century Engraving* (New York: New Trend, 1983), 35–45.
44. Merrill, *Wood Engraving and Wood Engravers*, 5.
45. *Ibid.*

under the New York end of the Brooklyn Bridge, and soon another engraver would pop in, and another, until nearly all the eight engravers who were to work on the page were collected there. Some solid and liquid food was obtained, and then we usually started up Broadway to study art in the saloons along the way. There were some really good paintings in a few of the places. By 6 o'clock we had returned to the shop, rested and ready for the work. I cannot recall that the engraved work suffered noticeably in quality.[46]

This anecdote makes it clear why illustration firms did not take on young women as apprentice wood engravers. The company of the male engravers was not considered at all appropriate for young ladies in the late nineteenth century. Instead, hundreds of women learned wood engraving at the Philadelphia School of Design for Women,[47] the Ladies School of Design attached to Cooper Union in New York, and similar institutions in Pittsburgh, Cincinnati, and other cities. The New York School of Design for Women opened in 1852 and combined with the newly founded Cooper Union in 1859. Over 200 women had learned wood engraving at the school by 1880, in addition to those who studied fine art.[48] Cooper Union discontinued wood engraving classes in 1890, when classes in pen and ink drawing suitable for photographic reproduction processes were substituted for them (fig. 5).[49]

The most famous wood engraver alumna of Cooper Union was Caroline Amelia Powell. Old School wood engraver William J. Linton taught wood engraving at the school when she was there. Powell described Linton's teaching at Cooper Union:

> He was a man who had much personal magnetism, and I remember how enthusiastic we girls were over him. His teaching was most irregular. Sometimes he would come for an hour or an afternoon every day in the week, and then we might not see him for a couple of weeks

46. *Ibid.*, 5–6.

47. Nina De Angeli Walls, 'Art and Industry in Philadelphia: Origins of the Philadelphia School of Design for Women, 1848 to 1876,' *The Pennsylvania Magazine of History & Biography* 117 (July 1993): 177.

48. Helena E. Wright, *With Pen & Graver: Women Graphic Artists Before 1900* (Washington, D.C.: Smithsonian Institution, 1995), 6–7.

49. Weitenkampf, *American Graphic Art*, 132; David Woodward, 'The Decline of Commercial Wood-Engraving in Nineteenth-century America,' *Journal of the Printing Historical Society* 10 (1974–75): 69.

Fig. 5. Women learning wood engraving at Cooper Union, New York, New York. Peter Cooper, the founder of the institution, is the man with the white beard at the left. About 1865. Reprinted from the *Magazine of Art* 40 (October 1947): 243. Reproduction courtesy of the National Museum of American Art, National Portrait Gallery Library.

or a month. We worked away more or less in the dark in his absence, but his visits were red-letter occasions, and his talks on engraving and art generally were most interesting and illuminating. He lent the class some of the priceless proofs of cuts in the *Illustrated London News* and other publications, some of them engraved when he was partner with Orrin Smith, the well-known English engraver. . . .They were beautiful proofs, and the most I learned at that time was from a faithful and incessant study of them.[50]

50. George Howes Whittle, 'Monographs on American Wood Engravers,' *The Printing Art* 31 (May 1918): 188.

On leaving Cooper Union, Powell tried to gain employment with *Scribner's Magazine*, but was told that her work was still not of the quality they required. Alexander W. Drake, art superintendent for the magazine, introduced her to Timothy Cole. Cole taught Powell the fine points of New School style engraving. She became a distinguished professional engraver elected to the exclusive Society of American Wood Engravers.[51]

Since the women engravers graduating from Cooper Union began their careers without the contacts in the field of illustration that men would have coming from the apprentice system, they needed aid from the school in beginning their careers. Cooper Union offered a special arrangement under which its alumnae and advanced students could execute commercial commissions in space provided at the school. The school arranged the commissions and took a percentage of the pay for them. When women finished their training and left Cooper Union and other schools, they did not work in male-dominated wood engraving shops. Most worked as free-lance engravers in their own homes.

A few women wood engravers ran their own shops which were staffed exclusively by women and took on female apprentices.[52] Sarah E. Fuller, mentioned above as the author of a wood engraving manual, attended the New York School of Design for Women before it merged with Cooper Union. She ran a wood engraving firm on Broadway in New York City in the 1860s.[53] Leila Curtis and her sister Mary Curtis Richardson both studied drawing and wood engraving at Cooper Union in 1858 and 1859, then returned to their home in California to found their own wood engraving studio.[54] They trained Eleanor Peters Gibbons, who also studied at Cooper Union. In about 1880 Gibbons became head of the firm where she had been an apprentice.[55]

51. *Ibid.*, 188–94.

52. Wright, *With Pen & Graver*, 7–8; Helena Wright, interview with author, November 29, 1994.

53. Wright, *With Pen & Graver*, 16.

54. Doris Ostrander Dawdy, *Artists of the American West: A Biographical Dictionary*, Vol. 1 (Chicago: The Swallow Press, Inc., 1974), 195.

55. Wright, *With Pen & Graver*, 16.

Ann Maverick (c. 1810–1863) was one of the first women wood engravers. She learned the art from her father, pioneer wood engraver Alexander Anderson (1775–1870). After the death of her first husband, Maverick supported her family by engraving. She married a second time, but when her second husband left her, she again turned to engraving for employment.[56]

Male free-lance wood engravers worked in their own homes just as the women did to provide engravings to various firms. They might at times briefly enter the shops of illustration firms or magazine wood engraving shops when the workload exceeded what the permanent engraving forces of these firms could produce.[57] Free-lance engravers negotiated their pay by the block, whereas shops paid their employees an hourly salary based on the speed and quality of their work. Merrill reported that in the 1880s the best were paid about forty dollars per week.[58]

Engravers who wished to rise in the field studied fine art to improve the quality of their engraving. For this reason, as well as because of their own interest in art, large numbers of wood engravers enrolled in fine art classes during the little leisure time allowed by their long hours of work. Despite a demanding schedule working for *Harper's*, Merrill took classes in drawing, composition, and painting at the Pratt Institute in Brooklyn and the Art Students League in New York City, where many wood engravers took classes.[59] In Boston, William B. Closson took evening classes at the Lowell Institute, where he studied drawing from classical casts and from life.[60]

Besides taking classes, Merrill painted and drew as much as he could on his own time. Two of Merrill's sketchbooks show that in

56. Stephen DeWitt Stephens, *The Mavericks: American Engravers* (New Brunswick, N.J.: Rutgers University Press, 1950), 73–74.
57. Kingsley, 'Life and Works,' 32–33.
58. Merrill, *Wood Engraving and Wood Engravers*, 4.
59. Merrill manuscript notes, Merrill Collection; Marchal E. Landgren, *Years of Art: The Story of the Art Students League of New York* (New York: Robert M. McBride and Company, 1940), 57.
60. Whittle, 'Monographs on American Wood Engravers,' *The Printing Art* 31 (April 1918): 118.

Fig. 6. *Levee, St. Louis*, watercolor sketch by Hiram Merrill, 1896. Hiram C.
Merrill Collection, Boston Public Library.

1896 he travelled around the United States sketching wherever he
went (fig. 6).[61] An urban scene is unusual, for Merrill enjoyed depicting rural and park scenes, and the urban realities of life in
Boston and New York seldom appear in his work.

Art clubs offered wood engravers a chance to extend their involvement with fine art. Elbridge Kingsley led a group known as
the Original Workers on Wood which included as members the
accomplished wood engravers John P. Davis, Frank French, and
Walter Monteith Aikman. The group, symbolized by a wood-
pecker, took sketching trips in the woods of New England.
Kingsley had fixed an enclosed wagon as a studio on wheels where
he could draw, paint, and engrave landscapes directly from nature.[62] Merrill was a member of the Salmagundi Club and the

61. Sketchbooks in Hiram Campbell Merrill Collection, Boston Public Library.
62. Frank French, 'Wood-Engravers in Camp,' *Century Magazine* 38 (April 1889):
569–75; Kingsley, 'Life and Works,' 97–124, 198–202, 230–32; Whittle, 'Monographs on
American Wood Engravers,' *The Printing Art* 31 (March 1918): 38; Whittle, 'Monographs
on American Wood Engravers,' *The Printing Art* 31 (June 1918): 277–78.

New York Water Color Club. Wood engravers also joined the Philadelphia Sketch Club and the Carbonari, a sketching club based in East Orange, New Jersey.[63]

As one might expect, the engravers' work reproducing illustrations was a heavy influence on the original art they produced. Merrill, for instance, greatly admired such illustrators as Edwin Austin Abbey. They were an influence both on Merrill's style and on his subject matter. His art, like many of the illustrations he engraved, tended to be anecdotal and descriptive, with an affinity for picturesque, rural themes with nostalgic associations. Merrill often painted the New England countryside where his mother's family lived and where he enjoyed vacationing. The illustrations Merrill engraved for the many travel articles in *Harper's* gave him a taste for distant, unspoiled locations. He later indulged this interest during long vacations in Europe. Merrill's work, like that of many illustrators, was allied with the vein of late-nineteenth-century culture which T. J. Jackson Lears calls anti-modern because it tended to cling to comforting tradition in the face of rapid social and economic changes.[64]

The engraving shop was not, however, the only influence on fine art made by wood engravers. Merrill's handling of color was much richer and more varied than one would expect of a person trained in a black-and-white field. The blue and purple shadows in his paintings from the teens and twenties reflect familiarity with the Impressionists and the American artists influenced by their work. The oil paintings that wood engraver William B. Closson made late in his career were often very painterly and atmospheric, qualities unexpected in the work of a wood engraver. Even as a wood engraver, however, Closson was well known for the subtle way in which he rendered softly shaded paintings.

63. Merrill manuscript notes, Merrill Collection; Whittle, 'Monographs on American Wood Engravers,' *The Printing Art* 32 (January 1919): 327.

64. Annette Stott, 'Dutch Utopia: Paintings by Antimodern American Artists of the Nineteenth Century,' *Smithsonian Studies in American Art* 3 (Spring 1989): 60; T. J. Jackson Lears, *No Place of Grace: Antimodernism and the Transformation of American Culture 1880–1920* (New York: Pantheon Books, 1981).

Wood engravers had the chance to study closely photographs of the art they reproduced, and sometimes the original art. For example, Closson was hired to engrave a painting by George Fuller, whose studio was in the same building as the engraver's studio. Closson said that 'I had the painting in my room during the time of engraving it, and before the work was finished I was completely in love with it and quite as completely won to admiration of Mr. Fuller as an artist and as a man.'[65]

Considering the modest artistic backgrounds from which most wood engravers came, their experience in illustration shops was probably more broadening than limiting. They saw great amounts of art on a daily basis, not only work done specifically as illustration, but fine art as well. Popular illustrated magazines such as *Century* and *Harper's*, as well as art-oriented magazines like the *Aldine*, included many articles about current art and the history of art in the United States and Europe. Working on the illustrations for such articles must have proved a fine education for the engravers.

For some people, however, reproducing the art of others could never be enough. Such artists as Willard LeRoy Metcalf, George Inness, Childe Hassam, and Thomas Moran served apprenticeships in wood engraving shops, but quickly left to become painters. These men were totally unsuited to the precise, black-and-white work of an engraver. They did, however, find that background in wood engraving was useful, since it offered an understanding of monochromatic design and gave them contacts in the publishing business.[66] Other artists remained in the engraving field for years before following the call of fine art. California-based painter

---

65. Whittle, 'Monographs on American Wood Engravers,' *The Printing Art* 31 (April 1918): 119.

66. Thurman Wilkins, *Thomas Moran: Artist of the Mountains* (Norman: University of Oklahoma Press, 1966), 20; Joni Louise Kinsey, *Thomas Moran and the Surveying of the American West* (Washington, D.C.: Smithsonian Institution Press, 1992), 79; The Corcoran Gallery of Art, *Childe Hassam: A Retrospective Exhibition* (Washington, D.C.: The Corcoran Gallery of Art, 1965), 11; National Gallery of Art/Detroit Institute of Arts, *American Paintings from the Manoogian Collection* (Washington, D.C.: National Gallery of Art, 1989), 194–96.

William Keith served an apprenticeship starting in 1856, duly became a wood engraver, worked for *Harper's*, and went into partnership with another engraver. By 1868 he had become disgusted with engraving and left the firm to become a painter.[67]

Like any new technology, the introduction of photographic methods of reproducing illustrations required a long period of experimentation before the costs were competitive and results were uniformly acceptable. Only then were these techniques widely adopted. The decline of wood engraving as a career was precipitated by a price war among illustrated magazines that broke out in the early 1890s as halftone and lineblock reproductions became more popular. By then these processes had become cheaper and more efficient. In 1893 a magazine could purchase a halftone for less than twenty dollars, while the cost of a full-page wood engraving was $300.[68] Halftones began to replace the comparatively costly and slow wood engravings for tonal illustrations. The photographic process of line block replaced engravings of line drawings.[69]

The camera gradually supplanted the New School of wood engraving as the medium for reproduction. Both the public and artists whose work was being reproduced demanded illustrations that were faithful to the original art, while the publishers required the cheapest and most time-efficient methods of reproduction. Despite complaints from the public (and from the wood engravers) about the dull, grey, lifeless appearance of halftones, the new technology prevailed.

When halftone and other methods of photoreproduction began to gain in popularity in the 1890s, the wood engravers who had remained in the profession found it collapsing beneath them. By 1894 *Harper's* let go about half of their engraving force.[70]

---

67. Eugene Neuhaus, *William Keith: the Man and the Artist* (Berkeley, California: University of California Press, 1938), 8–11; Brother Cornelius, *Keith: Old Master of California* (New York: G. P. Putnam's Sons, 1942), 11–12.

68. Frank Luther Mott, *A History of American Magazines, Vol. IV, 1885–1905* (Cambridge: Harvard University Press, 1957), 4–5.

69. Woodward, 'The Decline of Commercial Wood-Engraving,' 66.

70. Merrill manuscript notes, Merrill Collection.

Scores of engravers in the many illustration firms around the country lost their jobs and had a difficult time finding other jobs in the area of the arts. By 1900 there were still 145 wood engraving firms in the United States, but the work for wood engravers had shrunk considerably.[71] Opportunities continued to exist, primarily in the fields of advertising and catalogue illustration, but most engravers had to find other ways to support themselves.[72]

Skilled engravers were able to continue working for illustration houses by learning to perform the reworking required by the early halftone plates.[73] Merrill was one of those who learned to burnish the areas of the plate intended to print the darkest and to cut out the white areas in a process closely resembling wood engraving.[74] M. Lamont Brown, writing in *Penrose's Pictorial Annual* (a British publication for professionals in the business of reproducing illustrations), singled out Merrill as one of the finest halftone engravers in the United States.[75] Merrill and his colleagues found work on halftones dull and lacking in the happy camaraderie of the wood engraving shop. In 1900 Merrill began working at home and eventually left *Harper's* to work for Alexander W. Drake at *Century*.[76] To take a break from his work on halftones and to widen his artistic experience, Merrill took two long vacations in Europe. He made many drawings, paintings, and photographs, particularly in his favorite villages in Brittany.

Some engravers who could not get or did not want halftone work, went into other aspects of illustration house work or became illustrators.[77] One of these was Alice Barber Stephens, who

71. Sander, *Wood Engraving* (New York: Viking Press, 1978), 20.
72. William Gamble, 'Catalog Illustrations,' *Penrose's Pictorial Annual. The Process Year-Book for 1900. A Review of the Graphic Arts* 6 (1901): 1–2; Woodward, 'The Decline of Commercial Wood-Engraving,' 69–72, 77.
73. Woodward, 'The Decline of Commercial Wood-Engraving,' 70.
74. Merrill, *Wood Engraving and Wood Engravers*, 8; Whittle, 'Half-Tone Etching as a Fine Art,' *The Printing Art* 29 (June 1917): 261.
75. M. Lamont Brown, 'Process Work in the States,' *Penrose's Pictorial Annual. An Illustrated Review of the Graphic Arts. The Process Year-Book, 1901* 7 (1903): 101–3.
76. Whittle, 'Half-Tone Etching,' 259; Merrill, *Wood Engraving and Wood Engravers*, 8.
77. Whittle, 'Monographs on American Wood Engravers,' *The Printing Art* 33 (April 1919): 99.

after studying at the Philadelphia School of Design for Women, was a commercial wood engraver for about twenty years. In the 1890s she became a book and magazine illustrator and worked in that capacity for about thirty years.[78] Those with the best training in fine art, such as William B. Closson, frequently turned to painting or etching portraits and landscapes.[79] Wood engravers with little fine art training or ability had to look for work outside the arts. Less fortunate wood engravers, even some very skilled ones, were unable to find steady work and became aimless drifters.[80] They must have felt completely betrayed by their training in wood engraving.

Looking at the legacy of Merrill, Kingsley, and the other engravers, we can form a good idea of the training and experiences of New School wood engravers. They existed in a unique time that they saw as a golden age of illustration. They were the last manifestation of pure craft in a field that worked to communicate unique art to the public. Technology surrounded them, aided them, and eventually displaced them. In the end, the 'ruling machine' in the lives of the wood engravers was the camera. A few engravers fulfilled their dreams of becoming fine artists, but many more found their way into related commercial fields. The lot of the wood engravers was mixed, made up of drudgery, camaraderie, satisfaction, and disappointment. Judging from the attitude of Hiram Merrill, Elbridge Kingsley, and many of their fellow wood engravers, they were willing to take the good with the bad so long as they could exist in the world of art.

78. Wright, *With Pen & Graver*, 19.

79. Whittle, 'Monographs on American Wood Engravers,' *The Printing Art* 31 (April 1918): 122.

80. Whittle, 'Monographs on American Wood Engravers,' *The Printing Art* 30 (December 1917): 226, and (January 1918): 299.

John Sloan's Newspaper Career: An Alternative to Art School

ELIZABETH H. HAWKES

I N T H E 1890s aspiring artists often lacked the financial means to pursue conventional art training, which entailed lengthy study at American and European academies. For John Sloan (1871–1951), gaining employment as a newspaper artist served as an alternative art education. Sloan spent twelve years as an artist working for two Philadelphia newspapers, the *Inquirer* and the *Press*, with a brief three-month hiatus at the *New York Herald*. He began his first newspaper job in 1892 at the age of twenty.

SLOAN'S EARLY YEARS

John Sloan was born in the central Pennsylvania lumber town of Lock Haven. His family moved to Philadelphia when he was about six.[1] His father, a photographer and cabinetmaker in Lock Haven, hoped for a better business opportunity and found employment as a salesman in a stationery business. The Sloans lived

I wish to acknowledge the support of Helen Farr Sloan; the John Sloan Memorial Foundation; Harriet Memeger, Librarian, of the Helen Farr Sloan Library at the Delaware Art Museum; and Mary F. Holahan, Registrar, Delaware Art Museum.

1. Sloan was still in Lock Haven in April 1877. Betty Elzea, *The Wards and the Sloans: The Family Connection Between the Irish Firm of Colour Printers and the American Artist John Sloan* (Wilmington: Delaware Art Museum, 1990), 36.

ELIZABETH H. HAWKES is an independent curator from West Chester, Pennsylvania, specializing in American painting and illustration. She served as Associate Curator at the Delaware Art Museum and Curator of the Museum's John Sloan Collection. She was co-author of *John Sloan: Spectator of Life* (1988) and author of *John Sloan's Book and Magazine Illustrations* (1993).

modestly. His mother Henrietta, a former schoolteacher, nurtured her children's love of books and pictures. Though the family had little money, there were always books to read. As a child, Sloan exhibited a precociousness for drawing and decorated his copy of *Treasure Island* with ink drawings.[2] He perused copies of books lavishly illustrated by Walter Crane, George Cruikshank, and Gustave Doré, among others.[3] Sloan's later involvement with art and illustration can be traced to these seeds planted in his youth. In 1884 he entered Philadelphia's Central High School, a public school for exceptionally bright students, where he was a classmate of William Glackens and Albert C. Barnes. Sadly, his father's health failed, and at age sixteen Sloan had to quit high school to support his family.

Between leaving Central High School and getting a job at the *Philadelphia Inquirer*, Sloan worked as a book store cashier, a greeting card and calendar designer, and a freelance artist. He recalled: 'I sort of drifted into art as a way of earning a living.'[4] Having had little art schooling, he enrolled in a freehand drawing night class at Spring Garden Institute in 1890. He taught himself to etch by reading Philip Hamerton's book on etching and completed his first oil painting, a self portrait, in 1890 after reading a painting manual.[5]

THE *PHILADELPHIA INQUIRER* AND THE NEWSPAPER
BUSINESS IN THE EARLY 1890S

In 1892 the *Philadelphia Inquirer* hired twenty-year-old John Sloan to work as a newspaper artist. The paper's publisher James Elverson had bought the *Inquirer* in 1889 and had immediately

2. This copy of *Treasure Island* is in the John Sloan Collection, Helen Farr Sloan Library, Delaware Art Museum.
3. From John Sloan's autobiographical notes collected by Helen Farr Sloan in *The Poster Period of John Sloan* (Lock Haven, Pa.: Hammermill Paper Co., 1967), unpaginated.
4. Quoted in *The Poster Period of John Sloan*.
5. Sloan's copies of Philip Gilbert Hamerton's *The Etcher's Handbook* (London: Charles Roberson and Co., 1881) and John Collier's *A Manual of Oil Painting* (London: Cassell and Co., 1886) are in the John Sloan Collection, Helen Farr Sloan Library, Delaware Art Museum.

begun transforming the lackluster paper to appeal to a new larger readership. Elverson used Joseph Pulitzer's *New York World* as a model.[6] Pulitzer, an immigrant, had bought the *World* in 1883 and increased its circulation from 15,000 to 1,000,000 readers in only fifteen years. Pulitzer changed the content of the *World* as well as its appearance. Sensational headlines and pictures of news events caught the attention of potential buyers. Human interest stories, fashion, and fiction enlarged his base of women readers. Throughout America, newspapers followed the Pulitzer formula in an effort to attract readers and increase both circulation and advertising revenues.[7]

James Elverson lowered the price of the daily *Inquirer* to one cent (most papers in Philadelphia sold for two or three cents). Newsboys shouted out the headlines. Some *Inquirer* headlines from 1892 were matter of-fact: 'Arguing women's rights' and 'Substantial aid for Russians'; others were bizarre: 'She murdered her rival,' 'He held dynamite between his teeth,' and 'Killed herself by her own hair.'[8]

Like Pulitzer, Elverson targeted a new mass audience—an influx of Americans from farms and small towns, as well as European immigrants, who flooded Philadelphia as well as New York and other metropolitan centers, seeking jobs, housing, and a better way of life. The *Inquirer* prided itself on appealing 'to everyone and to every condition of life,' instead of catering to the educated male readers newspapers had relied on in the past.[9] Though battling a language barrier, foreign immigrants learned to read headlines and classified ads. In the ten-year period from 1890 to 1900, circulation figures of American daily newspapers doubled (from 8 million to 15 million). As readership increased, so did advertising by department stores and retail businesses seek-

6. From 1889 to 1892, the circulation of the daily *Inquirer* increased from less than 5,000 to 70,000. *Philadelphia Inquirer*, January 10, 1892, 4.
7. Pulitzer's chief competitor in New York City was William Randolph Hearst, who acquired the rival *New York Journal* in 1895.
8. These headlines appeared in the *Philadelphia Inquirer* in 1892.
9. *Philadelphia Inquirer*, December 16, 1894, 44.

ing to appeal to this new mass market. On each day's editorial page, the *Inquirer* proudly printed daily circulation figures in bold typeface with an accompanying statement: 'The Largest Circulation of any Republican daily newspaper in the United States,' thereby persuading advertisers that their ads would reach a large audience.

In January 1892, the month Sloan joined the staff, the *Inquirer* expanded its Sunday paper to sixteen pages. Elverson recognized the circulation potential provided by working people who had Sunday off (most Americans worked a six-day week). Reading the Sunday paper became a form of leisure and a family activity. In a headpiece for the 'Boys and Girls Page,' Sloan drew an attractive young mother reading the paper to her children.[10] The new Sunday *Inquirer* boasted of fiction by accomplished contemporary Americans such as Mark Twain and Bret Harte; a 'women's page' of fashion and how-to-do articles, for example 'Coming Styles in Bonnets' or 'Buying Groceries'; and a popular society page.[11] For children there were stories, puzzles, and a page of jokes and cartoons. In other words, the Sunday *Inquirer* had all the ingredients of a weekly magazine but cost only three cents in direct competition with ten- and fifteen-cent magazines.[12]

Appealing to working-class families as a serious readership was a cunning move. In the past newspapers had focused on male readers with articles about politics and business. But when department stores became major advertisers, newspapers changed focus and began targeting women readers. Clearly women, who oversaw shopping trips, made decisions about what clothes, furniture, and food to buy. The *Inquirer* reminded potential advertisers that 'the family man and the family woman' were the pay-

10. The drawing served as a headpiece for the 'Boys and Girls Page,' *Philadelphia Inquirer*, December 16, 1894, 30.
11. 'Each Sunday there will be a page devoted exclusively to matters of interest to women. These will be written, not for the wealthy few, but for the great mass of people who want helpful hints in housekeeping, dressmaking, cooking, etc.' *Philadelphia Inquirer*, January 10, 1892, 20.
12. The Sunday paper was advertised as 'a weekly illustrated magazine by the best authors that cannot be duplicated.' *Philadelphia Inquirer*, January 10, 1892, 20.

ing client.[13] Newspapers became influential forums for promoting new products. Soon advertising income surpassed subscriptions as the newspaper's chief source of revenue.

The *Inquirer* promoted its own services. During the recession of 1894 the paper argued that reading newspapers was good for business. An unsigned ad, now attributed to John Sloan, shows a comfortable family scene in which a businessman reads a newspaper, while his wife and children study books in their library. According to the picture's caption, the businessman confides: 'Yes, the times are pretty hard all over the country, but . . . I have plenty of work. . . . I attribute our good fortune to the fact that I have always kept abreast of the times.'[14] The meaning was obvious: businessmen should read the *Inquirer*.

In 1894 the *Inquirer* opened a new six-story office building in Philadelphia to house the editorial, business, and printing facilities. It was acclaimed as 'the most thoroughly equipped newspaper office in the world,' with a new press capable of printing 100,000 eight-page newspapers an hour.[15] The *Inquirer* published a picture of guests attending the opening celebration with an article describing how the picture was prepared. First, staff artists copied a photograph of dignitaries at the reception. On a rush job, several artists worked on different parts of a single drawing to meet the deadline. Within two hours the drawing was sent to the engraving room. It took only 3½ hours from the time the photograph was taken until the engraved plate was in the press ready to be printed. This was a phenomenal feat for the time.[16]

Recognizing that pictures sold newspapers, Elverson hired young artists to draw not only the daily political cartoon which had

13. *Philadelphia Inquirer*, December 16, 1894, 44.

14. *Philadelphia Inquirer*, May 20, 1894, 16.

15. *Philadelphia Inquirer*, December 16, 1894, 37. The *Inquirer* published a special supplement about the new building and the paper, see 37–44. The article announced that the new press was the largest and 'speediest' in the world and had safety guards to prevent loss of fingers, a common accident in the press room. It also noted that there were 250 incandescent lights in the business office and that 'bright-looking men of the nattiest-looking type' worked in the advertising office.

16. *Philadelphia Inquirer*, December 16, 1894, 1.

long been a staple in papers, but also pictures of news events, prominent leaders, fashion designs, and advertisements. But within a few years, due to technological advances, photographs could be printed on newsprint without the intervention of an artist.[17] Photographers quickly displaced artists. Newspapers' dependence on artists was a short-lived phenomenon lasting only about a decade.

WORKING AS A NEWSPAPER ARTIST

When John Sloan joined the *Inquirer* in 1892, the paper boasted that its illustrations were 'excelled by no newspaper in the country.'[18] Though this assertion was exaggerated, pictures were a prominent feature in the paper and drew the attention of readers eager to see as well as read the daily news, whether a fire in downtown Philadelphia, a trolley accident, or Benjamin Harrison's nomination at the Republican convention.[19] Newspaper artists sketched on the site, from photographs, or from descriptions received by telegraph, that were considered as timely then as television's live coverage is today.

Newspapers hired young artists with basic drawing skills and trained them on the job. There were at least five artists on the *Inquirer* staff when Sloan worked there. R. C. Swayze provided a daily political cartoon and also covered news stories; for example, his drawings of a tragic theater fire that killed six performers appeared in a front-page story. Harry Ponitz specialized in fashion illustration and copied photographs of people in the news, whether murderers or politicians.[20] Edward Davis, known today as the father of famous American painter Stuart Davis, also worked at the *Inquirer* for a few years before moving to the *Philadelphia Press*. Everett Shinn worked there briefly in 1894.

17. An article about tornadoes in the Midwest featured dramatic photographs of the storms. 'Tornadoes Caught by the Camera,' *Sunday Philadelphia Press*, June 18, 1899, 29.

18. *Philadelphia Inquirer*, January 10, 1892, 20.

19. For examples, see the *Philadelphia Inquirer*, June 11, 1892, 1; May 21, 1894, 1; and January 28, 1895, 1.

20. For a description of the paper's art department, a list of staff, and photographs, see *Philadelphia Inquirer*, December 16, 1894, 39, 40, 43. For drawings by Swayze and Ponitz, see *Philadelphia Inquirer*, April 28, 1892, 1, and February 14, 1892, 1.

Fig. 1. John Sloan (right) and other staff artists at the *Philadelphia Inquirer*, 1894. Photograph. John Sloan Collection, Helen Farr Sloan Library, Delaware Art Museum.

The art department manager Joe Laub designed headings, advertisements, and decorative borders.

These young *Inquirer* artists typically worked a six-day week sitting at drawing boards along a row of windows (fig. 1).[21] They joked together, argued about politics, and rushed to scenes of news-breaking events. Years later, Sloan recalled the camaraderie of his newspaper days: 'But we were as happy a group as could be found and the fun we had there took the place of college for me.'[22] Some

21. A photograph of Sloan seated at his drawing board appeared in the *Philadelphia Inquirer*, December 16, 1894, 38.
22. Sloan described the *Press* art department: 'a dusty room with windows on Chestnut

newspaper artists enrolled in night classes at the Pennsylvania Academy of the Fine Arts to augment their drawing skills. Sloan enrolled in a course where he drew from plaster casts of classical sculpture and briefly attended Thomas Anshutz's life drawing class. But he was frustrated by the Academy's classes. His newspaper experience provided real-life situations that art school did not. At work, he copied photographs of people, buildings, and events. He drew people on the street and in courtrooms or at sports events and charity balls. Copying plaster casts and nude models seemed contrived in comparison to drawing real-life situations. As a newspaper artist, Sloan developed a keen memory for what he saw, a useful skill when he became a painter.

Not all newspaper artists became painters. Swayze, Ponitz, Laub, and Davis from the *Inquirer* did not. Frederic R. Gruger, who worked for the *Philadelphia Press*, won painting prizes while studying at the Academy, but he became a successful magazine illustrator providing a steady income and comfortable life style for his wife and children. By contrast, Sloan, Shinn, Glackens, and George Luks all got their start working for newspapers and then went on to become respected painters.[23] Robert Henri, a young and dynamic artist, inspired them to paint. Before meeting Henri, Sloan was interested in becoming only a good illustrator, but Henri motivated him to get serious about painting.

Sloan's early drawings for the *Inquirer* were hesitant and not particularly distinguished, but his skill developed quickly. His portrait drawing of Charles A. Dana, editor of the *New York Sun*, published on the *Inquirer*'s front page (April 24, 1892), imitated the style of magazine wood engraving. According to the caption, Sloan copied Dana's 'latest photograph,' emphasizing the timeli-

and Seventh Streets—walls plastered with caricatures of our friends and ourselves, a worn board floor, old chairs and tables close together, "no smoking" signs and a heavy odor of tobacco, and Democrats (as the roaches were called in this Republican stronghold) crawling everywhere.' 'Artists of the *Philadelphia Press*,' *Philadelphia Museum Bulletin* 41 (November 1945): 7.

23. American writers Stephen Crane, Theodore Dreiser, and Lincoln Steffens began their writing careers as newspaper reporters.

ness of the image. Photographs of prominent figures, politicians, actors, and community leaders were kept on file in the art department for artists to copy. Another early assignment, an investigative story about recent boiler explosions in Philadelphia, showed the wreckage of a hotel destroyed by an explosion killing twenty-three people. Though an immature example of his work, the drawing captured the devastation of the scene. Sloan, however, was not particularly proficient at making rapid-fire drawings of action scenes—accidents, fires, and other catastrophes. On the other hand, Everett Shinn and William Glackens were adept at action work done under the heat of a deadline. Sloan's early assignments gravitated toward decorative headings and portraits of debutantes and brides for the Society page.

Sloan met Beisen Kubota, a Japanese artist who taught him how to sketch in brush and ink in the Japanese manner. This gave Sloan the impulse to adapt elements of the Japanese style, namely, asymmetrical designs, flat patterns, and crisp outlines in his newspaper drawings. Sloan's Japanese style was part of a broader movement, generally called the 'poster style,' that swept America in the mid-1890s. From about 1894 to 1899, magazine publishers issued colorful posters incorporating Japanesque design elements to advertise upcoming issues of their magazines. Sloan became the first artist to use the poster style for newspaper work in a drawing of spectators at a tennis match (June 10, 1894).[24] The composition differed radically from standard newspaper drawings. The figures of the men and women were reduced to flat black and white shapes in outline and were asymmetrically balanced by patterned areas (fig. 2).

Becoming his hallmark, Sloan's poster-style drawings appeared regularly in the *Inquirer* in 1894–95 accompanying feature arti-

24. Sloan's first poster-style drawing was published in the *Philadelphia Inquirer*, June 10, 1894, 12. In earlier literature concerning Sloan's newspaper work, another drawing of a tennis match, *On the Court at Wissahickon Heights*, is mistakenly identified as his first newspaper poster-style drawing and incorrectly dated February 12, 1892; the drawing was actually published June 13, 1894.

Fig. 2. John Sloan, *Tennis at Wissahickon*. Ink on paper, 6¹/₂ in. x 5 in. Published in the Philadelphia Inquirer, June 10, 1894. Delaware Art Museum, gift of Helen Farr Sloan, 1993.

cles, society reports, and fiction. For example, drawings depicted scenes at New Jersey seaside resorts (fig. 3), guests at the German-American Charity Ball held at the Academy of Music, and episodes from a short story, 'An Episode in an Artist's Life.'[25] By then Sloan was aware of Aubrey Beardsley's drawings in *The Yellow Book*, as well as posters by Jules Chéret and Edward Penfield.[26]

In 1895 Sloan gained his first national recognition when the *Chap-Book* and *Inland Printer* magazines featured his poster-style drawings. He also sent poster-style drawings to other privately printed 'little magazines'—*Echo, Gil Blas*, and *Moods*. While serving as art editor of *Moods*, a short-lived art/literary magazine published in Philadelphia, he produced a striking cover design. His consummate skill at abstract design, practiced in both his newspaper and magazine illustrations, informed his early paintings as in the deft composition for the restaurant scene, *The Rathskeller*, 1901 (Cleveland Museum of Art).

After four years at the *Inquirer*, Sloan moved to the competitor, the *Philadelphia Press*, where his friends William Glackens and Edward Davis now worked. Sloan wrote to Henri in December 1895 explaining his move: 'I have one wheel out of the rut, or at least into a shallower rut, I have left the Inquirer. . . . I am in better company and am getting more money. . . .'[27] He worked at the *Press* more than two years and then moved briefly to the *New York Herald* during the summer of 1898. The *Herald* hired artists to replace those sent to Cuba to cover the Spanish-American War. Sloan made drawings for stories filed by reporters about the war. Then, when the *Philadelphia Press* offered him a salary increase, Sloan returned to the paper in the fall to work on the Sunday Supplement. In an ad for the Supplement, the *Press* promised

25. *Philadelphia Inquirer*, July 22, 1894, 10; August 12, 1894; January 6, 1895, 20; and January 22, 1895, 3.

26. Two of Beardsley's drawings from *The Yellow Book* were reproduced in 'Porter's London Letter,' *Philadelphia Press*, February 10, 1895, 31.

27. Sloan to Henri, December 8, 1895, Robert Henri Papers, Beinecke Rare Book and Manuscript Library, Yale University.

Fig. 3. John Sloan, *On the Pier*. Ink on paper, 13 1/8 in. x 17 3/4 in. Published in the Philadelphia *Inquirer*, June 22, 1894. Delaware Art Museum, gift of Helen Farr Sloan, 1980.

'colored and photographic pages . . . without a rival in the great field of newspaper illustration.'[28] Sloan was hired to illustrate fiction, create children's puzzles, and design decorative borders.

When Sloan returned to the *Press* in 1898, the days of the newspaper artist were numbered. Newspapers were reproducing photographs regularly. Sometimes, both an artist and a photographer were dispatched to an assignment; if the photograph failed, the artist could supply the necessary drawing. By 1900 most newspaper artists had lost their jobs to photographers. Sloan hung onto his job at the *Press* until 1903, because he worked as a designer and illustrator for the Sunday Magazine Supplement, not as an artist-reporter.

Sloan employed different styles and experimented with color, ink, and crayon for the Sunday paper. He devised new contests, puzzles, and games to entertain children. In one contest, children colored pictures in the paper and sent them to the *Press*, where the one judged best was published and awarded a prize. Even this stimulated sales, because parents bought newspapers so their children could enter the contest.

Sloan's more imaginative and ambitious works for the *Press* were his full-page puzzle drawings printed in color, for example, the *Snake Charmer Puzzle* (May 5, 1901). The objective was to find a young boy playing the flute cleverly hidden in the design (fig. 4). Sloan's 'Word Charade Puzzles' offered popular entertainment. He drew a series of fifteen pictures each of which represented a word. An example was the letter Z followed by a sketch of a cat knocking over a bottle of ink; the answer was Zinc.[29] Readers responding with correct answers were listed in the next week's paper. Also, using his skills as a designer, Sloan made intricate decorative borders for pages of text and photographs.

Sloan also illustrated serialized fiction in the Sunday Supplement of the *Press*. His ink drawings for 'Jennie Baxter, Journalist' were done in a style reminiscent of nineteenth-century English

28. *Philadelphia Press*, December 25, 1898.
29. *Philadelphia Press*, November 1, 1903.

Fig. 4. John Sloan, *Snake Charmer Puzzle*, Philadelphia *Inquirer*, May 5, 1901.
Color line cut reproduction, 22 3/8 in. x 17 3/4 in. John Sloan Collection, Helen
Farr Sloan Library, Delaware Art Museum.

artist John Tenniel. Sloan's crayon drawings for short humorous pieces by John Kendrick Bangs and W. E. Norris were based on French prototypes by Honoré Daumier, Gavarni, and Jean Louis Forain (fig. 5).[30] Later, Sloan expanded his realist vision in the De Kock book illustrations, New York City etchings, and magazine illustrations for *McClure's* and *The Masses*.

Sloan lost his job at the *Press* in December 1903, when the newspaper stopped producing the Sunday Supplement, subscribing instead to a syndicated magazine. However, he negotiated with the *Press* to continue supplying 'Word Charade Puzzles,' which provided a modest, but steady, income. Sloan decided to move to New York City with his wife Dolly to work as a freelance magazine illustrator. His fellow newspaper artists and friends, Glackens, Shinn, Luks, Laub, and Davis had already moved to New York, as had Robert Henri. Losing his job provided Sloan with the necessary incentive to move. In New York Sloan earned his living first as an illustrator and later as a teacher, while he concentrated seriously on painting and etching.

What did Sloan gain from this newspaper experience? First of all, he had the opportunity to experiment with different styles, media, and subjects. He gained considerable skill as a designer of composition that transferred to his work as a painter and etcher. Also, he developed an eye for anecdotes in real life that made good, though unconventional, subjects for paintings: buying flowers on a rainy Easter eve (*Easter Eve*, 1907, private collection), children playing in the snow (*Backyards, Greenwich Village*, 1914, Whitney Museum of American Art), or spectators watching a hairdresser at work (*Hairdresser's Window*, 1907, Wadsworth Atheneum).

His newspaper experience nurtured his irreverent attitude toward the status quo, whether elitist leaders of the academic art establishment or narrow-minded party politicians. Sloan developed a healthy respect for his newspaper audience—the 'common man

30. See examples of the 'Jennie Baxter' and John Kendrick Bangs illustrations in *Philadelphia Press*, June 4, 1899, and November 8, 1903.

Fig. 5. John Sloan, *He Discusses Poets*, "The Genial Idiot" by John Kendrick Bangs, Philadelphia *Sunday Press*, October 18, 1903. Pencil and crayon on board, 25 x 19¹/8 in. Delaware Art Museum, gist of Helen Farr Sloan, 1980.

and woman,' whom he saw both as his subject and his audience. Finally, he learned that the power of the press could shape and influence public opinion. So, it is not surprising that when Sloan and his friends staged the historic 'Exhibition of the Eight' at the Macbeth Gallery in New York City in 1908—a show that changed the direction of American art—they welcomed the extensive press coverage.

Educating American Designers for Industry, 1853–1903

NANCY AUSTIN

MANY DISCUSSIONS of Postmodernism claim a radical historical break occurred after World War II when a new consumer society emerged defined by swings in fashion and styling, planned obsolescence, the pervasive use of advertising, and new national and international networks of distribution. Art historians who trace the prehistory of such a Postmodern society most often look to the theoretical work of the Frankfurt School. However, a growing body of interdisciplinary scholarship is documenting late eighteenth- and nineteenth-century examples of a familiar consumer society, focusing in particular on the complex nature of art production after the Industrial Revolution.[1] This paper examines the early history of

I would like to thank Caroline Sloat (AAS), Georgia Barnhill (AAS), Mark Brown (John Hay Library), and Carol Terry (RISD Library) for their helpful support.

1. Russell Lynes, *The Tastemakers* (New York: Dover Books, 1949); Neil McKendrick, 'Josiah Wedgwood: an Eighteenth Century Entrepreneur in Salesmanship and Marketing Techniques,' *Economic History Review* (2nd series, 12.3) 1960: 408–33; Mary Douglas and Baron Isherwood, *The World of Goods* (London, 1979); Elizabeth Wilson, *Adorned in Dreams* (Berkeley: University of California Press, 1985); Colin Campbell, *The Romantic Ethic and the Spirit of Modern Consumerism* (Cambridge: Basil Blackwell, 1987); Daniel Miller, *Material Culture and Mass Consumption* (Cambridge: Basil Blackwell, 1987); Grant McCracken, *Culture and Consumption* (Bloomington: Indiana University Press, 1988); Martyn Lee, *Consumer Culture Reborn* (New York: Routledge, 1993).

NANCY AUSTIN is a member of the Department of Industrial Design, Rhode Island School of Design. Work on this paper was partially funded by a RISD Faculty Development Grant.

design education in the United States as a tool for articulating how thoroughly the industrial revolution, and the expanding markets its success depended upon, transformed the dialectic between fine art and consumer culture. One might say, how thoroughly the art of commerce transformed the commerce of art. The origins of this transformation are in the late eighteenth and nineteenth centuries, and not in the decades after 1945.

The design school is a key site from which to study this transformation. It is a new institution of the nineteenth century. Unlike the much older Academies of Art which Nikolaus Pevsner has documented,[2] the design school's reason for being was to fill the needs of the new industrial manufacturing class. However, this basic goal became imbedded in the complex cultural agenda of providing an art museum for the good of the people, to educate taste. The typical history of the nineteenth-century museum focuses on the museum's new civic role in the city and the contribution of wealthy, often female, philanthropists.[3] Counterbalancing this view, it will be argued here that the primary need to train designers for industry was the engine carrying the art museum in its train—and not the other way around.

It is important to remember that the designer is not a new kind of laborer in the nineteenth century. A designer is someone who creates models or working prototypes for serial reproduction. The designer as a type of laborer predates the industrial revolution for the simple reason that the division of labor to mass produce products preceded mechanization. There is nothing *intrinsically* modern about separating the process of design and/or model-making from the process of fabrication.[4] For example, in the seventeenth and eighteenth centuries the French court created such a demand for luxury goods that a manufacture

2. Nikolaus Pevsner, *Academies of Art* (Cambridge: Harvard University Press, 1940).

3. See, for example, Kathleen D. McCarthy, *Women's Culture: American Philanthropy and Art, 1830–1930* (Chicago: University of Chicago Press, 1991).

4. Edward Lucie-Smith, *A History of Industrial Design* (New York: Van Nostrand Reinhold, 1985). This is one of the best overviews of serial producation before mechanization.

was established where urban artisans worked from designs provided by famous painters; the process of making was divided into component tasks which were then duplicated by hand.[5] This is not that dissimilar from the method of production of ancient Greek pottery.[6]

However, until the eighteenth century the scale of most industries seldom required more than one craftsman to be responsible for every stage of production. For example, it is not until 1750 that the division of labor in the British pottery industry was extensive enough that we find workers specifically described as modelers.[7] The organization of labor in the British calico printing industry (pattern drawer, block cutter/engraver, printer) did not change from the late 1600s until the introduction of water-powered roller printing machines in 1796, when the engraver and printer were rendered redundant while opportunities for pattern drawers increased.[8] The industrial designer is unique *only* in creating working prototypes for serial reproduction *by machines*. But within the context of machine production, in many industries beginning in the 1830s, the industrial designer became more valuable to the manufacturer. As Adrian Forty has put it, 'the successful design . . . released the machine's capacity to make a profit.'[9]

5. This history is noted even in the founding document of the Rhode Island Art Association, *Circular and Constitution* (Providence: 1853), 10–11. See note 18 below. It would appear that there is an ongoing history of art that incorporates the realities of mass or workshop production, but this sort of history is not tolerated by historians who emphasize the self-generated achievement of individual genius.

6. R. M. Cook, *Greek Painted Pottery* (London: Methuen & Co., 1972), 270–74.

7. Adrian Forty, *Objects of Desire* (London: Thames & Hudson, 1986), 34. Forty reports that in 1769 a modeler was paid twice the wage of a skilled craftsman. Forty (p. 44) quotes Marx arguing that mechanical production only completes what the division of labor began, that is, the source of alienation begins with the division of labor and not mechanization per se. See also Dietrich Rueschemeyer, *Power and the Division of Labor* (Stanford: Stanford University Press, 1986).

8. Forty, 44–51.

9. Ibid., 58. This process has accelerated today with the advent of computer-aided, rather than mechanical, tooling. For example, the clothing company, Benetton, maintains no inventory but, via computer, tracks changing taste and can redesign its merchandise and distribute it worldwide in seventeen-day cycles. See Stephen Bayley, *Commerce and Culture* (London: Design Museum, n.d.), 113–15.

As more industries were mechanized in the 1830s, the industrial designer took on an ever more important role mediating between the manufacturers' striving for profit-making designs and the growing numbers of consumers desiring differentiated products. The industrial designer's function was to create design differentiation for a class society where exercising taste was one of the most important modern vehicles for the social construction of identity. The design school can be seen as a contested cultural site for the representation of cultural capital after industrialization introduced mass consumption on an unprecedented scale. Historians and critics on the left and the right have been strangely unwilling to consider consumer products in terms other than the negative one of commodification or with moralizing cries for a lost pre-industrial past. Usually these campaigns have gone on under the guise of advocating 'real needs' or 'good taste.' These lacunae will not be addressed until more cultural historians confront the issue of education, the commerce of art, and mass consumption.[10]

Although the design school was new, it carried with it a residue of the artisan tradition. Industrialization proceeded slowly and continued to incorporate older forms of production. Throughout the nineteenth century many mechanized consumer product factories continued to include hand-based, artisanal labor. The designer and model-maker was the aristocrat of these artisans, but all skilled laborers were a class above the new factory proletariat. The design school's clientele was the factory-based, skilled artisan (fig. 1).

In the United States, a national discussion on the importance of training American designers for industry began in the 1850s and culminated during the period from 1867 to 1887 with the ambitious establishment of design schools in manufacturing cities across the country. Based on British, French, and German

10. The absence of industrial design history from practically all American universities (including those with politically-engaged cultural studies programs) represents a failure to address one of the quintessentially modern cultural practices.

Fig. 1. A Gorham artisan etching silver, c. 1892. The worker shown here is carefully painting a nonconductive resist varnish over a perviously drawn pattern or scene. After this, the piece would be dipped into an acid bath to corrode away the unvarnished surface leaving the varnished design in relief. The protective varnish woiuld then be removed, and the pattern would stand out in relief. This process might be repeated three to four times to achieve a pattern of varying depth. Women with drawing and painting skills were considered most likely to succeed at this task. *Women's Work at the Gorham Manufacturing Company*, 1892. Brown University Library.

precedents, these new American design schools resulted from the intersecting interests of businessmen, manufacturers, artists, wealthy female patrons of the arts, and educators who have left us a largely-untapped literature elaborating a belief in the uniquely modern possibilities of artistic design for industry, and the necessity of educating (equally) men and women for this new practice.

The Rhode Island School of Design (RISD) can serve as an exemplary case study of an evolving design school during this pivotal period. A Rhode Island design school was first proposed in December 1853 by a consortium of Rhode Island manufacturers whose objective was to overcome foreign competition by establishing a local source of designers. Their two-pronged approach was to train designers for local industry and, as an integral part of this process, to establish an art gallery or museum as a repository of correct artistic or symbolic capital. That is, the design school's mission was not only to transmit skills in a vocational setting, but also to display and legitimate what Pierre Bourdieu has called cultural capital—the taste of one economic class.[11]

The manufacturers' efforts were hindered by the Civil War. RISD was incorporated in 1877; classes were first held the next year. The first objective of the school was: 'The instruction of artisans in drawing, painting, modeling, and designing, that they may successfully apply the principles of Art to the requirements of trade and manufacture.'[12]

In one sense, the mission of the entire school was to train designers for industry. But the second companion mission was to establish an art collection to wrap around this other goal (fig. 2). In practice, a thriving fine-art curriculum came to coexist with that devoted to applied and mechanical arts. The early treasurer, William Weeden, thought of it this way:

> The day pupils are generally in independent circumstances, and are being educated for artists, amateurs, and buyers of works of art, and elegant objects. We need a higher standard at large in the community, in order that true design may be appreciated. . . . The evening pupils are chiefly sons of mechanics and working men. . . . These pupils will naturally become workers in design applied to arts and manufactures.[13]

11. Pierre Bourdieu, 'Cultural Reproduction and Social Reproduction,' in *Power and Ideology in Education* (New York, 1977), 487–510; and Pierre Bourdieu, *Distinction: A Social Critique of the Judgement of Taste* (Cambridge: Harvard University Press, 1984).

12. *Circular of the Rhode Island School of Design* (Providence: J. A. & R. A. Reid, 1878), 5. The three-point statement of mission has been reprinted each year to the present, and is one of the two commonly-used references for explaining RISD's origins.

13. Elsie S. Bronson, 'The Rhode Island School of Design; a Half-Century Record 1878–1928' [typewritten manuscript], Archives, Rhode Island School of Design, Providence, 13. Elsie Bronson presented her completed manuscript to the London pub-

Rhode Island School of Design

The objects of this school are : —

FIRST. The instruction of artisans in drawing, painting, modelling, and designing, that they may successfully apply the principles of Art to the requirements of trade and manufacture.

SECOND. The systematic training of students in the practice of Art, in order that they may understand its principles, give instruction to others, or become artists.

THIRD. The general advancement of public Art Education, by the exhibition of works of Art and of Art school studies, and by lectures on Art.

Fig. 2. The Rhode Island School of Design's founding mission statement. *Circular of the Rhode Island School of Design, 1878–79*, 5. RISD Archives.

Fig. 3. Mary F. Richards, "A Corner of the Lecture Room," *Circular of the Rhode Island School of Design, 1891–92*, 5 RISD Archives.

Or, as the first school headmaster stated in a letter:

> We have now considered the school chiefly in a practical and technical sense, that is, in the relation which it bears to the great needs of a manufacturing community; but it is to be hoped that it will be successful also in interesting ladies and gentlemen of taste and leisure in art studies; for their attendance will increase its power and broaden its influence in another very important direction. I hardly need to urge the claims of art as a delightful occupation for leisure hours.[14]

The student body at RISD as a whole was a microcosm of the social relations of late nineteenth-century Providence.

Until World War I, it was ambiguous whether consumer product design was the dog wagging the tail of the fine arts, or if it was the other way around (figs. 3, 4, and 5). This was resolved by the late 1920s as RISD prepared to become a nationally

lishing firm of Brown, Shipley & Co. in August 1932, but then history has never been published. The Bronson manuscript remains the only detailed history of the institution.

14. Ibid., 11.

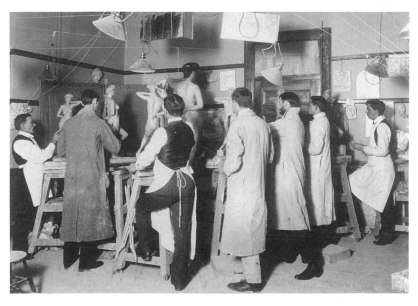

Fig. 4. Male students drawing the female nude, c. 1900. RISD Archives.

accredited, degree-granting institution of higher education. A RISD brochure announced: 'The School of Design is not, it must be understood, a trade school.'[15]

The impetus for a Rhode Island design school lay in its status as an important nineteenth-century industrial center. Indeed, Pawtucket, Rhode Island proclaims itself to be the birthplace of the American Industrial Revolution because of the successful cotton mill Samuel Slater ran there on the banks of the Blackstone River beginning in the 1790s. Slater's water-powered

15. RISD brochure, 'Mechanical Design Department' (Providence, n.d. [1928]). This transformation was noted by former RISD President John R. Frazier (1955–1962) in his internal report from the mid-1950s entitled, 'An Inquiry Into Causes that Brought About Changes in Curricula and Educational Standards in Rhode Island School of Design.' The concluding remarks were: 'It seems certain that the intent of the founders relative to the training of artisans as outlined in the first purpose of the charter has been completely disregarded in the drive to bring the Day School to college level. It is equally certain that if the founders had desired to establish a technical school at college level this intention would have been clearly stated. On the other hand, times change, and institutions with them. Charters, like constitution, have to be interpreted in the light of clear and present conditions.'

Fig. 5. Textile studio, c. 1913. RISD Archives.

mill spawned other local textile and companion tool-making factories. By the 1820s and 1830s the factory system had become
firmly established in Rhode Island with major industries of metal
trades, tooling, rubber, textiles, jewelry, and silversmithing. One
of these early silversmithing firms was located in Providence and
had been founded by Jabez Gorham, whose son John Gorham
entered the firm in 1841, forming J. Gorham & Son.[16] In the
1850s and 1860s John Gorham transformed the small, fourteen-
employee company into the world's largest manufacturer of silverwares. In 1878—the year RISD opened—the British Parlia-
ment noted that a Providence company had now outproduced
the total annual British production of fine silverwares.[17]

But from the vantage point of 1850 the two problems facing a

16. Charles H. Carpenter, Jr., *Gorham Silver, 1831–1981* (New York: Dodd, Mead &
Co., 1982), 28–32; 40–41.

17. This also was the year John Gorham was ousted from the company due to his personal bankruptcy; see Carpenter, 91–93.

Fig. 6. The Gorham factory buildings at Canal and Steeple Streets, Providence, R.I. before 1890. The First Baptist Church is at left.

manufacturer like John Gorham were technology and a limited product line. Gorham wanted to introduce mass production machinery into the production of flatware, to utilize lathe-production for hollow ware, and at the same time to offer more products ornamented in more styles. In 1852 John Gorham went to London, Birmingham, Manchester, and Sheffield to study British production and design methods. Gorham's diaries are at the John Hay Library and record his search. He spent his days apprenticing in factories anywhere he could get in, learning production methods, interviewing designers and artisans. Gorham returned to Providence with a basic design library and study collection, the first American steam-powered drop press for the manufacture of flatware, and the detailed information gleaned from the factory artisans about the British design schools that were in the founding circular of the Rhode Island Art Association one year later (fig. 6).

The Rhode Island Art Association was born out of the need of Rhode Island manufacturers to produce local designers for their factories. As stated in the thirty-page circular written December 1853:

The manufacturer is now discovering that the best price, the most certain market, the greatest demand for each and all of the fabrics he is producing; are in some strange way connected with the highest taste shown in their design, the greatest harmony in their proportions, or the greatest beauty in their embellishments. It is not enough that his article is as good as or as useful as his rival's: if it is more beautiful it secures the prize, if it is less it is driven from the field. . . .

The history of manufacturing advance in all countries demonstrates . . . the advantage be found on the side of that where elements of beauty in design, or elegance in decoration, enter most largely. Nor only where material and workmanship are equal is this true, but even where advantage in these points lies with the less elegant and ornamental product. . . .

[Now] the designs come to us by steamer in a few days after their production, and are immediately copied here; and thus our own goods are in the market before the foreign consignments can reach us through the slower sailing vessel—so that it will be time enough to produce our own designs, when this cheap piracy becomes no longer possible. . . .

The only way to avoid dependence upon others for many articles that we know how to make ourselves, is not be dependent upon them for our ideas of beauty, and for that subtle regulator of trade—our popular taste. The only way to possess these in any degree, is to cultivate them through all the means and appliances in our power; and one of the best of these means, has been shown by the experience of those nations most largely interested; to be the establishment of a good School of Design, with a subsidiary Gallery of Art. . . .

It is a scheme that does not confine its benefits to one or two chosen classes in the community, but it reaches throughout the whole. The report of the Sheffield School, for 1849, shows that its pupils came from every walk, and what is of more consequence, that many of them returned again to the employment in which they were originally engaged. . . .

Nor are *men* alone interested in its plan.—There is a large and fast increasing number of *women*. . . .

We would say but a few words in conclusion. The Society presents itself to the public as a willing agent in a great public movement. It relies upon the past history of manufactures, when contrasted with the present, to prove the remarkably successful results of a cultivation of Art but very recently undertaken with reference to their improvement. It accepts as its field the two departments that have been found so well adapted to this end: an Art Museum and a School of Design mutually connected. It believes that the advantages they offer are especially valuable to a people like our own, and are applicable to both sexes, and to almost every age, and occupation; and grounds its hope of success on the intelligent conviction of every reader, that *as Art advances, manufactures and commerce advance with it.*[18]

Almost 150 manufacturers, merchants, lawyers, academics, clergy, and other men signed the circular establishing the Rhode Island Art Association. The treasurer was John Gorham. It seems likely that Gorham, as the first to introduce steam power into a city factory, the first to sublet power to other manufacturers, the first with the drop press, and the first to compile a major design library, was a major force behind this document with its articulation of a design school and companion museum.[19]

The Rhode Island Art Association was incorporated in May 1854. In January 1858 the Association submitted a formal proposal for the establishment of a Rhode Island School of Design. The document's authors asserted that the goal of such a school was 'the supply, to the manufacturer, of a kind of labor essential to his success, and hitherto but scantily furnished. . . . He will be enabled to make goods, which, with his present system of dependence on imported models and designs, he cannot now manufacture. He will soon begin to originate patterns, and can enter

18. *Circular and Constitution of the Rhode-Island Art Association* (Providence: Knowles, Anthony & Co., 1854), 6–7; 16–18, 22–23. A copy of this document is at the Rhode Island Historical Society Library. The meeting was announced in the *Journal* December 7, 1853, page 2, and reported on December 13, 1853, page 2. The meeting was held in Franklin Hall, Market Square.

19. *American Sterling Silver Ware: A Sketch of the Gorham Manufacturing Co.* (Providence, n.d. [1876]), 5. Rider Collection, John Hay Library, Brown University. At this time, the Gorham plant extended between North Main and Canal Streets, and Steeple and Friend Streets.

more successfully into competition with the foreign producer.'[20]
They noted that free or almost free schools of design already had
been opened in Boston, New York, Philadelphia, and Baltimore
with good results. For example, in Philadelphia, the best patterns
for house papers now were produced locally by designers who
were graduates of the program.

After the Civil War, design education became the battle cry of
manufacturing centers nationwide. In 1870 Massachusetts—on the
petition of merchants and manufacturers—passed a law requiring
every city with more than 10,000 people to provide day and
evening classes in industrial and mechanical drawing for people
over the age of fifteen.[21] In the decade around the 1870s eleven
American design schools, including RISD, opened their doors.

George Ward Nichols summarized this sentiment in his 1877
book, *Art Education Applied to Industry*:

> The broad meaning of the term 'art education' has not always been
> understood. It is most often used in its relation to the fine arts of
> painting, sculpture, and architecture, as if these higher arts and the
> industries were not mutually dependent, or as if the boundary which
> is supposed to separate them were not, . . . constantly invaded. . . .
> But the term 'art education' is used here in the largest sense. It
> means artistic and scientific instruction applied to common trades
> and occupations, as well as to the fine arts. It means the educated
> sense of the beautiful is not the special property of one class but that
> it may be possessed and enjoyed by all.[22]

Nonetheless, basic divisions in the curriculum track at RISD were
class-based. The bifurcation within the freehand division between
painters and designers signified a class difference between the
wealthy, often female, amateur/collector and the working artisan.

20. *School of Design Proposed to be Established by the Rhode Island Art Association*
(Providence, n.d. [1858]), 2–3. [Petition to the General Assembly, 1858.]

21. Walter Smith, the key advocate in Massachusetts, wrote: 'Among all the educational movements which have arisen in this country during the 1870s, none has seemed
so completely in harmony with the spirit of the times as education in the elements of
industrial arts.' Walter Smith, *The Masterpieces of the Centennial International Exhibition*
(Philadelphia: Gebbie & Barrie, n.d. [1876]), II: 497.

22. George Ward Nichols, *Art Education Applied to Industry* (New York: Harper &
Bros., 1877), 4.

But there also was a hierarchy within the design curriculum. For example, *industrial* design meant something specific. Courses in industrial design at RISD were part of a freehand drawing curriculum that featured sequential specialization leading to a concentration in either 'flat' or 'round' design; machine design was part of a separate curriculum based on mechanical drawing. That is, industrial design was identified from the beginning with the primary production of commodities and not with the design of the machines that facilitated production (fig. 7).[23]

It is usual to begin the history of RISD with its incorporation on April 5, 1877, through the efforts of the ladies of the Rhode Island Centennial Committee, who returned from the 1876 Centennial exhibition with a surplus of $1,675 which they used to found a school of design.[24] It is tempting to see this construction of origin as part of the process by which the primary goal of educating designers for industry became feminized and clothed in the more socially-accepted and gentle pursuit of a disinterested aesthetic education with a museum as the primary institution and the training of artisans as a secondary adjunct.

This was probably not the intention of the most important of these Centennial Committee women, Mrs. Jesse Metcalf, who actively managed the daily operation of the school for nearly two decades until her death in 1895 (fig. 8).

During her tenure, Mrs. Jesse Metcalf actively recruited reproductions of 'great art' in the form of casts and photographs, as well as industrial and mechanical models. These would form the core of a 'well chosen industrial museum.'[25] In 1885 RISD

23. What became an independent degree in Industrial Design in the 1940s developed out of this freehand, rather than the mechanical, drawing curriculum.

24. *An Address Commemorative of Jesse Metcalf and Helen Adelia Rowe Metcalf* (Providence: Snow & Farnham, 1901); Bronson, 5–6; McCarthy, 64–65. McCarthy writes: 'Another institution in which women figured prominently, the Rhode Island School of Design Education (RISDE) [sic], became one of the country's major educational institutions in the fine arts. . . . Like many of its sister chapters, the Rhode Island group exceeded its fund-raising quotas for the fair, leaving a tidy nest egg of $1,675, which was promptly invested in a new art school. . . . While Metcalf took care of the daily administrative chores, her husband assumed the financial burdens.'

25. *RISD Yearbook* (Providence: J. A. & R. A. Reid, 1888), 20.

FREE HAND DEPARTMENT.

Painters, Engravers, Jewelers, Chasers, Silversmiths, Designers, Wood Carvers, Etc.

FIRST YEAR.	FIRST TERM.	Drawing from Geometrical Solids. Historic Ornament (cast). Perspective.		
		PAINTERS.		**DESIGNERS.**
	SECOND TERM.	Ornament, Light and Shade. Perspective. Harmony of Color.		Elements of Growth in Design. Plant Analysis. Style and History of Ornament. Ornament, Light and Shade.

SECOND YEAR.	FIRST TERM.	Still Life, Black and White. Detail Antique Figure. Antique Figure. Perspective Shadows. Still Life—Color. Architectural Orders.	**DESIGNERS IN THE FLAT.** Historical Ornament. Architectural Orders. Detail Ornament from the Antique. Harmony of Colors.	**DESIGNERS IN RELIEF.** Historical Ornament. Architectural Orders. Detail Ornament from the Antique. Detail Figure from the Antique.
	SECOND TERM.	Antique Figure. Anatomical Rendering of same. Human Head from Life. Human Figure from Life, Pen and Ink for Processes of Reproduction.	Designs in Black and White and in Color for Wall Paper, Oil Cloths, Prints, Carpets, etc.	Antique Figure. Anatomical Rendering of same. Designs for Jewelry, Wood Carving, Stone Cutting, Furniture, etc.

Composition, including Costume and History of Ornament, continued through the Second and Third Years.

THIRD YEAR.

COURSES IN DRAWING, PAINTING, MODELING, WOOD CARVING AND DESIGN.

Fig. 7. The designer's education was conceived as part of the Freehand Department which had a course of study distinct from the Mechanical Department *Circular of the Rhode Island School of Design, 1878–79,* 5. RISD Archives.

MECHANICAL DEPARTMENT.

Draughtsmen, Pattern Makers, Carpenters, Machinists, Etc., Etc.

FIRST YEAR.

FIRST TERM.

Free Hand Drawing from Geometric Solids.

Graphical Geometrical Problems.

Orthographic Projections from Models, Patterns and Machine Parts.

SECOND TERM.

Intersection and Development.

Use of Color and Brush.

Isometric Projection

Working Drawings.

SECOND YEAR.

CARPENTERS AND BUILDERS.	MACHINISTS & PATTERN MAKERS.
FIRST TERM. Architectural Details. Plans and Elevations. The Orders. Perspective.	Study of and Drawing from Successful Machines. Reduction of Free-hand Sketches to Working Drawings.
SECOND TERM. Framing Plans. Building Construction. Strains and Weights. Roof and Floor Trussing.	Study of Assembled and Detailed Drawing. Study of Mechanical Movements. Designs of Cams, Gearing, etc. Elements of Machine Designs.

THIRD YEAR.

SPECIAL COURSES . . . MATHEMATICS, MECHANICS AND DESIGN.

considered itself lucky to obtain 'charts, models, and casts of ornaments similar to those used in the Prussian Art Industrial schools.' After Mrs. Metcalf's death, her husband—a prominent Rhode Island woolen manufacturer—funded an addition to the school to house gallery space. For another decade the gallery exhibitions ran the gamut from the nude figure, to work in metal, relief modeling, architectural drafting, book illustration, to the ever-popular machine design (fig. 9).

It should be borne in mind that in 1891, when a benefactor named Albert Jones left $25,000 for the purpose of founding an art museum in the city of Providence, RISD's ability to claim the bequest was contested because its purpose was to train artisans.[26] RISD's lawyer countered that it had already established a museum as part of its course of instruction, and that there was really nothing to *prohibit* considering a school of design to be the same as an art institute.

Helen Adelia Rowe Metcalf's role in getting RISD off the ground was pivotal. (Her descendents have continued their financial support to this day.) What this matriarchal lineage has obscured is the fundamental economic incentive of manufacturers like John Gorham and the other members of the Rhode Island Art Association in setting the wheels in motion. What the manufacturers needed was the designer who could release 'the machine's capacity to make a profit' in the new era of a consumer society. With industrialization, the designer becomes a key social actor whose history has been almost constantly obscured by the attention paid his more famous counterpart—the progressive artist. America may have industrialized early, but studying the cultural implications of mass production is still virgin territory.

In the dialectic between the production of fine arts and design-driven consumer goods, design education had as much to

26. Newspaper clipping dated October 1891, Archives, Rhode Island School of Design. The 1895 *RISD Yearbook* announced receipt of the bequest 'by decree of court.'

Fig. 8. Frank W. Benson, Portrait of Mrs. Jesse Metcalf. Museum of Art, Rhode Island School of Design, gift of Mr. William C. Baker, Mrs. Manton Metcalf, Mrs. Stephen O. Metcalf, and Mrs. Gustav Radeke.

Fig. 9. The Waterman Galleries, Rhode Island School of Design, opened 1897. Early exhibitions indiscriminately combined the display of machine designs, figurative sculpture, paintings, and studies for jewelry and other decorative arts. RISD Archives.

do with reasserting a standard of taste based on the fine arts as it had to do with the skill-based needs confronting manufacturers. In the late twentieth century, as we continue to adjust to the experience of industrialization and the growth of consumption on an ever more enormous scale, it is as important as ever to explore the dialectic between fine art and mass consumption, and to be alive to how we use the power of our knowledge of art to educate. In the modern period, the prestige of fine art must be read within the context of mass consumer culture.

Art Museum Schools: The Rise and Decline of a New Institution in Nineteenth-Century America

JOYCE WOELFLE LEHMANN

PROFESSIONAL ART SCHOOLS formally attached to fine art museums emerged as a new institution for training aspiring artists during the nineteenth-century industrialization and urbanization of America. In the school unit of the early institutions, training usually was limited to one general studio art program where persons seeking careers in fine art, commercial art, or teaching received instruction together. Study focused on copying the museum component's typical collection of classical European paintings hung in tightly-packed multiple rows alongside antique statuary casts. This new hybrid institution provided a structured alternative to the apprentice system, and became a significant presence in the nation's growing urban centers well before college art departments developed as primary suppliers of post-secondary art training.

JOYCE WOELFLE LEHMANN is an educational historian and an adjunct professor in education at SUNY Oswego. In addition to a Ph.D. from SUNY University at Buffalo, she holds a Masters degree in art from Rochester Institute of Technology. Her doctoral dissertation on the history of the art museum school formerly attached to the Albright-Knox Art Gallery in Buffalo, served as a resource for the gallery's Anniversary Exhibition 'An Historical Survey of Painting in Buffalo,' March to June 1987.

Her other interest is inequality perpetuated through educational processes, and she edited a book of migrant farmworker oral histories for Cornell University in 1990. The book was a major resource for the 'Goin' North' exhibition held at the Rochester Museum and Science Center, July 1991 to June 1993. Currently, she is expanding this research to include the organizations that serve migrant farmworkers in Wayne County, New York.

These school-museum combinations apparently had been adapted from three separate European models. The first model, academies offering fine art instruction, existed in Europe since the sixteenth century as an option to customary apprenticeship training in master artists' studios. These academies had been founded by collaborating guilds that not only sought to increase artists' status by raising their occupation above the level of a craft, but had an added missionary goal of reforming taste and dominating the aesthetic environment.

Another model was the Louvre in France, the first public fine art museum to exhibit masterpieces formerly seen only in private, royal, or church collections. The Louvre opened in 1793, and began to provide limited art training assistance by the early part of the next century. Although the museum offered no accompanying instruction, its galleries were reserved in alternating five-day periods for art students to study and copy the collection. At that time in nineteenth-century Europe, usually only industrial design museums such as those in the German cities of Dresden, Stuttgart, Leipzig, and Hanover were establishing formal affiliations with training schools—a combination that was a third model for the new American institution.[1]

In the process of transposing these European models, the word 'academy' became a general designation for various forms of newly emerging art organizations in America. Samuel F. B. Morse noted this confusing practice during the early 1800s while serving as president of the National Academy of Design in New York and offered this definition: 'An Academy of Arts is an Association of Artists for the purpose of instruction and exhibition.' Although Morse's description fit some academies, others were founded as

1. Peter Marzio, 'A Museum and a School,' *Chicago History: The Magazine of the Chicago Historical Society*, VIII (Spring 1979), 20. Ephraim Weinberg, in 'Art Museums, Museum Schools & Studio Related Programs,' *Report of November 1982 AAMD Education Committee Conference* (Savannah, Ga.: Association of Art Museum Directors, n.d. [1983]), 33. Blanche Carlton Sloan and Bruce R. Swinburne, *Campus Art Museums and Galleries* (Carbondale, Ill.: Southern Illinois University Press, 1981), 8–9. Lois Marie Fink and Joshua C. Taylor, *Academy: The Academic Tradition in American Art* (Washington, D.C: Smithsonian Press, 1975), 14, 22.

schools only or museums only, and many were organized and managed by the social or financial elite of a community who often were not artists. For example, the Buffalo Fine Arts Academy, now known as the Albright-Knox Art Gallery, was founded by a combination of civic leaders and artists in 1862 as a museum only. Another exception was the Pennsylvania Academy of the Fine Arts, reputedly the nation's oldest continuing art organization. Although the 'instruction and exhibition' part of Morse's definition did fit this institution, it had been founded in 1805 by community leaders, not artists; however, the governing board which oversaw both the museum and school subsequently arranged for a group of distinguished painters, sculptors, engravers, and architects to actually administer the school.[2]

This new institution of art school-art museum had various organizational structures. Usually a professional art school was founded as a supplement to the museum's primary functions of collection, conservation, and exhibition, and was the accepted interpretation of an educational function specified or implied in a museum's charter. For example, the Buffalo Academy added a school in 1878, sixteen years after the museum's founding. Sometimes, however, these symbiotic school-museum combinations developed in another way: the art school came first, with the museum added afterward often as an appendage in the form of a teaching collection, as happened at the Art Institute of Chicago. Still another pattern was the founding of institutions to function dually as mutually supporting units of school and museum, which was the intention at the Pennsylvania Academy of the Fine Arts.[3] In addition, a rare approach to creating a museum school occurred toward the end of the century when the University of

2. Winifred E. Howe, *A History of the Metropolitan Museum of Art* (New York: Columbia University Press, 1913), 1:52; Weinberg, 'Art Museums, Museum Schools & Studio Related Programs,' 37.

3. Theodore Lewis Low, *The Educational Philosophy and Practice of Art Museums in the United States* (New York: Teachers College, Columbia University, 1948), 9–26; Joyce Lehmann, 'The "Albright Art School" of the Buffalo Fine Arts Academy: 1887–1954' (Ph.D. diss., SUNY Buffalo 1984), 29; Marzio, 'A Museum and a School,' 21; Weinberg, 'Art Museums, Museum Schools & Studio Related Programs,' 34.

Cincinnati transferred its School of Design to the Cincinnati Museum Association.

It appears, then, that these school-museum institutions did not follow any consistent form, but evolved in different ways from a general expectation that a fine art museum and a professional art school were an appropriate combination in nineteenth-century America. Similarities did exist, however, in the types of classes available at these schools. In addition to instruction in drawing from antique statuary casts and the copying of paintings in the affiliated museum's collection most schools added clay modeling and sculpture. Also included at some institutions was a frequently controversial class in painting or drawing from a live model—usually taught separately for male and female students (fig 1). Some schools offered mechanical drawing, woodcarving, fabric design, and similar specialized subjects, a practice which became increasingly common by the end of the century. Tuition ordinarily could be paid by the term or the month for each individual course, with an overall registration fee of five to ten dollars.[4] Most museum schools provided scholarships for those unable to pay, with some customarily reserved only for males. Often scholarships were provided by art patrons whose attitude of Christian stewardship toward their wealth prompted its use for others but did not necessarily preclude the conspicuous and often less altruistically-motivated philanthropy that sometimes underwrote early museums and the affiliated schools.[5]

Several conditions in America during the nineteenth century evidently supported the development of art school-art museum combinations. Probably the most important was the need for student access to original art at a time when travel even for short distances generally was difficult, reproductions were scarce and usually of poor quality, and copying the art of the past was a necessary

4. Lehmann, 'Albright Art School,' fns. 170 and 171; Peter Marzio, *The Art Crusade: An Analysis of American Drawing Manuals, 1820–1890* (Washington, D.C.: Smithsonian Institution Press, 1976), 7–9.

5. Low, *Educational Philosophy and Practice*, 1; Florence Levy, ed., *American Art Annual*, XII (Washington, D.C.: The American Federation of Arts, 1915), 235.

Fig. 1. The Art School—Portrait Class from *Report Covering the Year 1910, The Buffalo Fine Arts Academy, Albright Art Gallery* (Buffalo, N.Y. 1911). Photograph courtesy of the Albright-Knox Art Gallery Archives, Buffalo, New York.

part of art training.[6] Additional factors relating to art school-art museum combinations reflect complex and contradictory attitudes toward fine art relating to industrialization and urbanization during this period. The deeply-imbedded Puritan tradition that considered fine art 'useless' and relegated it to a peripheral position in education began to be replaced, at least temporarily, by the belief that the study of fine art could be a valuable and transferable basis for improving industrial product design. Along with this were prevalent beliefs that the presence of cultural institutions could attract new industry and business to urban centers, and that public access to fine art per se would serve as an uplifting moral force for urban workers. At mid-century, other circumstances developed to further support school-museum combina-

6. Kenyon Cox, 'Museums of Art and Teachers of Art,' in *Art Museums and Schools—Four Lectures* (New York: Chas. Scribner's Sons, 1913), 62; Marzio, 'A Museum and a School,' 23.

tions. American manufacturers were embarrassed by the poor quality of their products at the 1851 Exposition of the Industry of All Nations held in London's Crystal Palace. This, together with the upcoming Centennial Exposition in Philadelphia, prompted those who previously had been interested in industrial arts education to found the Pennsylvania Museum and its School of Industrial Arts in 1875, with the expectation that industry in the city and state would benefit. The Pennsylvania institution was modeled after the South Kensington Museum of London, now the Victoria and Albert Museum, which had been established a year after the Crystal Palace Exposition to encourage industrial arts there.[7]

The practice of displaying industrial products alongside fine art in museum galleries further linked museum and business interests. These mixed exhibitions and a growing obligation felt by museums to offer instruction in applied arts continued through the last half of the nineteenth century and into the first decades of the twentieth century and appeared to be part of a pragmatic justification for public funding of fine art museums.[8]

Also evidently contributing to art school-art museum combinations were private expectations of the mercantile and industrial nouveau riche who generally provided the wealth to found and sustain early cultural institutions. As a group, this new American gentry was much more city-oriented and pro-urban than most Americans; and having increased leisure, many sought ways to test and prove their social capabilities in a manner acceptable to their peer group. In addition to political, charitable, and other pursuits, some also developed mechanisms within cultural institutions for establishing social status—in art museums usually through self-perpetuating governing boards. Ordinarily these were composed of successful merchants, industrialists, bankers,

7. Sherman E. Lee, 'Art Museums and Education,' in *Art Museum as Educator*, ed. Barbara Newsom and Adele Z. Silver (Berkeley: University of California Press, 1978), 23; Jane H. Shikoh, '"The Higher Life" in the American City of the 1890s' (Ph.D. diss., New York University, 1972), 275.

8. Low, *Educational Philosophy and Practice*, 26–27; Newsom and Silver, eds., *Art Museum as Educator*, 7.

and urban professionals who were able to use their positions to sponsor elaborate social occasions at the museum, as well as to provide studio art classes that acceptably filled the premarriage years of adolescent daughters of social elites or those aspiring to that status. Some skills in sketching and drawing by the daughters and young members of this group were expected, and it was fashionable after a formal or informal 'graduation' to belong to art clubs sometimes affiliated with the art school or museum.[9]

It may be that pressure to provide some suitable training within a protected cultural setting for all women was an additional impetus in establishing museum schools, as female students often were the majority at many of these schools. The Buffalo Academy's school, for example, had female enrollments ranging from an original two-thirds to one-half during the first few decades of its existence. Although some women at that school and elsewhere may have been elite dilettantes, it seems evident that many of them were serious students. Art training was needed by women expecting to teach in public schools, by participants in the arts and crafts movement, and by those involved in cottage industries. Professional training also was important for women in sectarian and utopian communities that marketed products such as Oneida Community tableware, as well as for those in art potteries, like Rookwood in Cincinnati, that developed after the Civil War. Some of the products exhibited in the women's pavilion at the 1876 Centennial Exposition in Philadelphia were outstanding, especially hand-carved furniture produced by several Cincinnati women who had been taught by wood-carving faculty at the University of Cincinnati School of Design. Apparently, as a result of the success of this exhibition, a lively debate arose about whether furniture or ceramics offered greater promise for the employment of skilled women. This seems remarkable at a time when women could enter London's Royal Academy only by sub-

9. Shikoh, 'The Higher Life,' 377–78; Francis J. Walter, 'A Social and Cultural History of Buffalo, New York, 1865–1901' (Ph.D. diss., Case Western University, 1958), 165.

terfuge and were actually excluded from enrolling at the French École until the end of the nineteenth century.[10]

Accompanying the factors that supported founding of art school-art museum combinations was an optimistic and, perhaps, naive spirit of social reform and competitive civic-mindedness that developed in America during the nineteenth century. This, together with sufficient wealth to support it, led Americans to establish multitudes of community, regional, and national organizations to provide culture, education, recreation, social welfare, religion, and community life in new urban centers. Amidst this phenomenon, where the didactic urge was strong, the art school-art museum combinations flourished.[11]

Typical comments relating to the value of these art schools during the final decades of the century appeared in the 1879 annual report of the University's School of Design in Cincinnati just preceding its transfer to the city's museum. For example, one person stated:

> I am informed by a member of a leading publishing house, that, within the last ten years, a marked change has taken place in the book trade of the city. There is a largely increased demand for illustrated works, and a much greater refinement of taste displayed in the choice of such, not only in regard to the illustrations themselves, but even to the style of binding and finish. This change, my information says, is directly traceable to the influence of the School of Design. An examination of any show-window in the city will reveal the same thing. In no specialty is the change more marked than in that of wall papers and wall decorations, to which the school has given particular attention of late years. In fact all the industries of Cincinnati in which artistic decoration is employed to enhance the value of the manufactured article are indebted to this school, not merely for the general improvement of taste, but for the education of many of the skilled artisans who produce the work.[12]

Commercial interests also increasingly seemed to be served at

10. Lehmann, 'Albright Art School,' 70; Robert Vitz, *The Queen and the Arts: Cultural Life in Nineteenth-Century Cincinnati* (Kent, Ohio: The Kent State University Press, 1989), 4, 191–94; Fink and Taylor, *Academy*, 33, 62.

11. Walter, 'Social and Cultural History of Buffalo,' i.

12. College of the City of Cincinnati. Ninth Annual Report for the Year Ending December 31, 1879; Cincinnati Museum Association 1884–85 Report, 7.

the school attached to Buffalo's art museum. Although the fine arts aspect never became eclipsed, toward the end of the nineteenth century its director stated that training there was intended for

> Artistic workers in iron, brass and bronze, gold and silversmiths, jewellers, decorative house and sign painters, ornamental wood workers, designers of dress goods, upholsterers, wall-paper designers, carpet and oil-cloth designers, stained-glass workers, lithographers, engravers, printers, florists, stone-cutters, masons and monumental designers, mechanical and architectural draughtsmen, illustrators, artists and sculptors.[13]

In addition, a history of the Art Institute of Chicago indicates that courses offered there before the turn of the century included architecture, newspaper illustration, and wood carving along with drawing, painting, sculpture, and anatomy. Although the theory still existed that basic fine arts training was directly applicable to designing practical objects, particularly textiles, carpets, wallpaper, crockery, glass, and jewelry, this 'derivative philosophy' began to be questioned. As pressure mounted for even more practical courses, the emphasis gradually centered on originality in industrial design itself; and by the 1920s the Art Institute had recognized the split and established an industrial arts curriculum leading to a degree.[14]

This increasing tendency toward practicality no doubt created philosophical incompatibility between some art schools and the affiliated museum; however, changes leading to the decline of these combined institutions already were occurring by the final decades of the nineteenth century. Colleges and universities had begun adding art departments, often aided by donated campus art collections that sometimes rivaled or surpassed those in public art museums. Also, credentialing and accreditation movements were growing, and the value of a standardized degree from an accredited institution tended to diminish the appeal of art education offered by a specialized postsecondary museum school.[15]

---

13. Clipping from *Express*, February 2, 1896, in Art Students' League of Buffalo Scrapbook of Newspaper Clippings, 1896–1909, 75–76.

14. Marzio, 'A Museum and a School,' 45.

15. Lehmann, 'Albright Art School,' 166; Marzio, 'A Museum and a School,' 46.

Furthermore, after 1900 most fine art museums developed new educational philosophies directed at interpreting museum collections for the general public. This included planned spacing and explanatory labeling practices, docent guides, lectures, publications, and other extension services often coordinated through an education department; and the new educational activities usually covered in the museum's general budget tended to supersede its commitment to separately subsidize a postsecondary school as an educational function.[16]

An additional development was a significant change in American art styles generally traced to the 1913 Armory Show in New York City. This show, considered the 'watershed' between classic, academic art and new contemporary styles, affected methods of art instruction as well as altering museum collection patterns — often leading to more specialized acquisitions and elimination of the antique statuary casts or decorative friezes that constituted the core of many early museum collections. Somewhat preceding the Armory Show, and accelerating during the decades that followed, the old practices of copying masterpieces and drawing from plaster casts gradually were replaced by art instruction emphasizing creativity and individuality, with the result that proximity to an art museum seemed less important.[17]

In the same period, better traveling conditions facilitated visits to more-distant collections, and increasingly refined photographic and printing techniques improved the quality of reproductions available for classroom teaching. Also, the use of art school-art museum combinations as social arenas by urban elites began to diminish when studio art training became less fashionable for its younger members and alternative educational and career opportunities seemed to interest the group more.[18]

This combination of circumstances led some museum schools to develop cooperative arrangements for standardized degrees at

16. Lehmann, 'Albright Art School,' 176.
17. Joshua C. Taylor, 'The Art Museum in the United States,' in *On Understanding Art Museums*, ed. Sherman E. Lee (Englewood Cliffs, N.J.: Prentice Hall, 1975), 38.
18. Lehmann, 'Albright Art School,' 175–76.

nearby colleges and universities, while some others became individually certified through specialized accrediting organizations such as the National Association of Schools of Art; however, many ended their museum affiliation by transferring into higher education institutions. Outcomes for some art schools that ended their museum affiliation after the mid-twentieth century were: the Albright Art School merged into the Art Department at the University of Buffalo in 1954; Herron School of Art merged into Indiana University at Indianapolis in 1967; Dayton Art Institute closed in 1974; and Columbus College of Art and Design became independent in 1982.

The institutional union of a professional art school with a fine art museum, which seemed appropriate in nineteenth-century America, had become almost an anomaly in the middle of the twentieth; and by the closing decade of the current century, only an estimated dozen schools continue their museum affiliation. Among them are the Art Institute of Chicago, the School of the Boston Museum of Fine Arts, the Art Academy of Cincinnati, Cranbrook Academy of Art, Corcoran School of Art, and The Pennsylvania Academy of the Fine Arts School.[19]

Persons associated with the remaining institutions express concern about this continuing trend toward separation and its possible adverse effects on the training of artists, art historians, and art instructors. Their concern is that art schools not affiliated with a museum tend to depend on book illustrations, slides, or other reproductions, thereby minimizing the important experience of studying original art that usually is taken for granted in the art school that is combined with an art museum.

Despite changing conditions that precipitated the movement's decline, these combined institutions still are considered valid; and

19. Bret Waller in 'Art Museums, Museum Schools & Studio Related Programs,' 22, 23; Lehmann, 'Albright Art School,' 16; the author gratefully acknowledges telephone conversations during April 1993, with Roy Slade, President of Cranbrook Academy of Art; Bret Waller, Director of the Indianapolis Museum; and Ephraim Weinberg, former Director of The Pennsylvania Academy of the Fine Arts School.
20. Marzio, 'A Museum and a School,' 20, 49, 50.

the belief continues that this relationship is essentially invigorating. In a history of the Art Institute of Chicago, Peter Marzio writes that the presence of an excellent art collection makes the educational experience richer and deeper; and regardless of differing purposes and difficulties innate to the relationship, a strong bond persists between a museum and an art school. He suggests that 'perhaps a feeling for art itself is the cohesive force.' Marzio apparently speaks for the art schools still affiliated with a museum when he indicates that 'This belief in the value of art, past or present, has been the cornerstone of the school-museum relationship, and despite the eroding force of numerous problems, an essential strength remains.'[20]

CHRONOLOGY

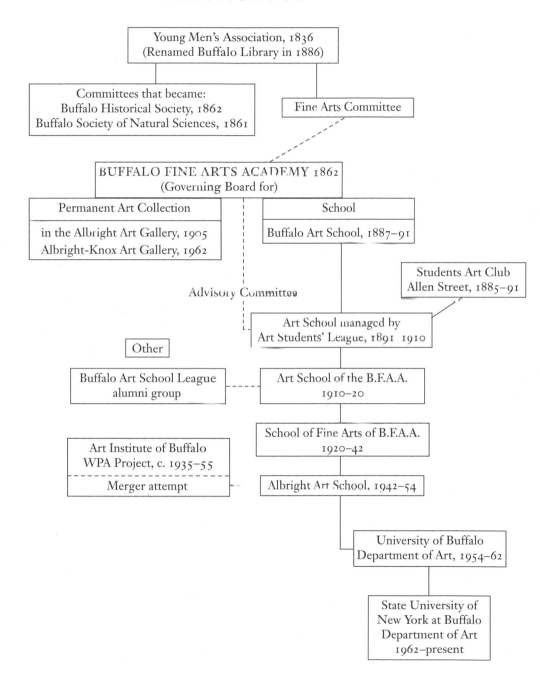

Young Men's Association, 1836
(Renamed Buffalo Library in 1886)

Committees that became:
Buffalo Historical Society, 1862
Buffalo Society of Natural Sciences, 1861

Fine Arts Committee

BUFFALO FINE ARTS ACADEMY 1862
(Governing Board for)

Permanent Art Collection

in the Albright Art Gallery, 1905
Albright-Knox Art Gallery, 1962

School

Buffalo Art School, 1887–91

Students Art Club
Allen Street, 1885–91

Advisory Committee

Art School managed by
Art Students' League, 1891–1910

Other

Buffalo Art School League
alumni group

Art School of the B.F.A.A.
1910–20

School of Fine Arts of B.F.A.A.
1920–42

Art Institute of Buffalo
WPA Project, c. 1935–55

Merger attempt

Albright Art School, 1942–54

University of Buffalo
Department of Art, 1954–62

State University of
New York at Buffalo
Department of Art
1962–present

Index